TORPEDOED DREAMS

A Love Story in Letters

Clive Ball

Cover picture by Marion Moss

By the same Author

SEVEN YEARS WITH SAMANTHA
Around the World in a Vintage Austin Seven

TORPEDOED DREAMS

A love story in letters

Clive Ball

I am sailing, I am sailing,
Home again 'cross the sea;
I am sailing stormy waters
To be near you, to be free.
(© Sutherland Brothers)

First Printing: October 2014

ISBN 978-0-9941972-1-4

Bryn y Pia Publications
117 Darlington Road
Darlington WA 6070
Australia

brynypia@iinet.net.au

Contents

Background   11

Early Letters   21

Courting Days   56

Engagement   66

Marriage   75

War   85

Parenthood   102

A Dance with the Duchess   124

A Narrow Escape   136

Last Voyage   146

Tragedy   160

The Aftermath   185

Appendix   194

Glossary of Welsh Terms   199

Acknowledgements

My grateful thanks go to Marion Moss for the cover picture; to Gavin Sutherland for permission to quote the verse from *I am Sailing*; to P Andrews and the ADCC (Qld) website for permission to quote the poem *In Memoriam*; to Karie Aszkielowicz for reading the draft manuscript and offering suggestions; and to my wife Sheila for her forbearance while I was writing and revising the story.

Thanks also to Wikipedia for numerous WW2 references; the UK National Archives for their comprehensive records of the wartime movements of Merchant Navy Vessels; and Ancestry.com for information from the American shipping records.

Except where otherwise credited, the photographs are from my own collection.

Preface

Some years ago, when I was clearing the contents of my mother's house, I found a suitcase full of miscellaneous old letters. I had begun burning them before I realised that many of them were the correspondence between my parents, from the beginning of their courtship until my father's heroic death in 1944, and that I was destroying family history. Of course, I stopped my vandalism immediately and rescued as many as I could, together with some relevant ones from other members of the family.

Reading the letters more thoroughly later, it occurred to me that I had the material to write a unique love story. Further research provided some missing pieces of the jig-saw puzzle to fill in the background of the 1930s and early 1940s, to which I've added anecdotes from my mother and other family members, and photographs from my collection.

I was only 2½ years old when my father died, and my memories of him are very limited. Writing this story has been a cathartic experience and has taught me a lot about a kind, loyal, decent man who loved my mother dearly. All my parents wanted was the chance to lead a normal, happy family life together, but it was denied them.

Darlington
Western Australia
October 2014

Introduction

Beryl and Leonard had known each other since their school days. Deeply in love and married for a mere 6½ years, they spent less than a year of that time together in total because of the demands of Leonard's work as a radio operator in the British Merchant Navy. Aged only 33, his life was ended by a German torpedo in 1944.

The tender letters they wrote to each other in neat copperplate handwriting tell most of the tale. It is a testament to their love for, and devotion to each other, set against the period from the Great Depression to World War 2 from their perspective. They were just two people among the millions whose happiness was destroyed by the War.

In loving memory of Beryl, and of Leonard, the heroic father
I barely knew.

To my dear children Melissa and Peter; and grandchildren
Issy, Ava, Brody, and a fourth due soon.

Background

The river Teifi rises north of Tregaron in the heart of Wales, collecting in the Teifi Pools before flowing some 75 miles south-westward in a graceful arc through an area of outstanding natural beauty. It meanders leisurely along broad meadowed valleys between rolling hills, and rushes down pretty wooded gorges, to empty into the sea near Cardigan. For most of its length it forms the boundary between the counties of Ceredigion and Carmarthenshire. Two small towns which straddle its banks about eight miles apart are Llandysul and Newcastle-Emlyn, from which two young people were to meet and be engulfed by their star-crossed destiny.

Beryl was born in Newcastle-Emlyn on October 20 1911. Her father, Jack Parkington, was an electrical engineer from Ipswich, Suffolk. Jack had been contracted to install an electricity supply in the town, where he met his wife Annie and never left. Beryl had one sibling, a younger brother Tom. She had an enquiring mind and once jumped off the coal shed holding an open umbrella to see if she could fly! A bright student with a range of interests, she took an active part in the life of the community, acting in plays, singing in concerts and *eisteddfodau* and participating in the many religious festivals which were a feature of those days.

Leonard was born in Llandysul on November 6 1910. His London-born father Fred Ball, a master painter, glazier, carpenter, gardener and artist, had married a local wife Rachel, and settled in the town. An older sister Maggie, a younger sister Gertie, and a younger brother Raymond completed the family.

According to relatives, Leonard was born with a "caul" over his head, which was regarded superstitiously as a sign of good luck, and an indication that he would not suffer death by drowning. In addition he contracted, and recovered from, diphtheria in childhood (a vaccine for this potentially lethal disease wasn't developed until the 1920s.) One day Fred, catching Leonard and his pals skinny-dipping in the Teifi, chased him home stark naked – although the boys had been bathing in a shallow part of the river, Fred was concerned about the treacherous pools and currents further downstream.

The district was predominantly Welsh-speaking. Leonard and Beryl both spoke Welsh, as did their mothers; neither of their fathers did – being Victorian Englishmen, it probably would never have occurred to them that they could learn! – so English was the language generally spoken at home. Most of the population was religious in those days, reinforced by the community: both families were committed Christians, attended churches regularly and genuinely practised their beliefs. As Annie and Rachel each had nine siblings, Beryl and Leonard both had many relatives living nearby.

The families were well respected in the district, but not particularly wealthy. Though Jack, an accomplished engineer, worked hard, he had the attitude of an enthusiast and was never overly concerned about money, much to Annie's chagrin. Fred, Rachel and Maggie ran the Rock Hotel, a five-bedroomed guest house where teaching staff at the local County School often stayed. Later, Fred, Rachel and Gertie found employment at Llandrindod Wells, about 50 miles away, leaving Maggie to run the hotel at Llandysul with Raymond, who was still at school.

Senior Class at Llandysul County School in 1928. Leonard back row, 11th from left. Beryl front, 1st left. Edmond Swete, behind Beryl, taught French, boarded at the Rock Hotel, and married Leonard's sister Maggie.

Torpedoed Dreams

The country's economy was still floundering after World War 1, with the Great Depression to come. Times were hard for most of the population. Many of the everyday things we take for granted nowadays would have been unimaginable then. People made do and scraped by on next to nothing. Our modern indulged teenager simply didn't exist – young people were expected to act like adults and pull their weight.

Leonard and Beryl met at Llandysul County School, which both had passed the entrance exam or "scholarship" to attend. He was smitten with her from an early age, whereas she thought he was "a bit silly". Leonard was popular, played soccer and cricket, went fishing for trout and salmon in the Teifi, joined the Scouts (he was rated on his enrolment card as *Good, keen and attentive*), enjoyed photography and cycling in the countryside as hobbies, and generally helped to run the hotel. Often not a diligent student at school, he was inclined to play tunes on banjo strings stretched under the desk when bored.

Beryl was also popular but more academically minded; she wrote stories and poetry, joined the Girl Guides, played the piano and enjoyed hockey and tennis. She travelled to and from school daily on the little GWR train with its cream and brown carriages, that puffed its way up the Teifi Valley from Newcastle-Emlyn. Leonard used to try to win her affection in ways such as dismantling the apparatus after a chemistry lesson, or taking photographs of her and her friends. When the train's smoke could be seen approaching in the afternoon, he often carried her school bag down the hill via the short-cut through the fields to the bridge, where they would part company.

The Great Depression began just as Leonard and Beryl were finishing their secondary education. Unemployment was extremely high all over Britain, especially after the New York stock market crash in October 1929, reaching 70% in some country areas in the early 1930s. Many young people had to leave home to find work.

From early in its development, radio was recognised as a useful means of communicating with ships, and a few were fitted with experimental equipment. After several maritime disasters culminating in the 1912 loss of the *Titanic*, to which the nearby *Californian* did not render assistance due to her radio being shut down for the night, it was realised that for radio to be a real aid in the safety of life at sea, all ships must maintain continuous "radio watch" for distress signals.

Laws were enacted to compel all the bigger ships to carry radio equipment, and also sufficient radio operators to maintain a 24-hour watch, which usually meant three. Their prime purpose was the preservation of life at sea during times of distress.

All communication in those days was by Morse code, a combination of dots and dashes. There were early technical limitations to speech transmission, also Morse could be read more reliably under conditions of poor reception or static.

Leonard had dabbled with radio as a hobby and decided to make it his career. Leaving school in May 1928 without taking the Senior School Certificate exam, he attended the Wireless College in Colwyn Bay, North Wales. He easily passed the entry test in English and Arithmetic, and trained for nine months as a Wireless Operator. He boarded at the College and was able to defer his fees until he started earning.

Courtesy Peter J. Robinson

Rachel, ever solicitous about Leonard's welfare, sent him small amounts of pocket money from time to time.

Rachel and Gertie to Leonard.   *Rock Park Cottage,*
Llandrindod Wells.
(Undated, late 1928).

My Dear Boy,
Just a word with the usual. I wonder how you are getting ready for the Exam – I hope everything will be all right. I am sending 2/6 extra this week for you to buy pencils and rubbers or whatever you will need.

Let me know how you are getting on during the week – a line or two will do, not a polished letter.

Gertie came on Tuesday. She looks well. I think we can get her a job at the Baths. We've been very busy there clearing away a tree that fell down in the big wind last Sunday. There will be enough firewood for a twelve-month.

Dad is very busy too between the Baths and the Water Board. Millward is ill so Dad had to meet the Councillors on Thursday, but they were quite pleased with everything.

Now Gertie is going to write a line to finish, so ta-ta, with the best of luck next week. Don't get flustered if you can help it.

Your loving Mam XXX

Dear Leonard,

Just a line to wish you the best of luck in your exam. I'm sending you a "lucky charm" to see if it might bring you luck! No more now.

Love from all, Gertie XXX

Leonard passed the exam, gaining the 1st Class PMG Certificate with technical knowledge and a proficiency in Morse Code of 25 words per minute. After they had completed the course satisfactorily, the Marconi company offered secure employment in the Merchant Navy for the College's trainees, a great advantage when so many people were jobless.

A photo taken in February 1929 shows him in Merchant Navy uniform. He commenced as 3rd Radio Officer on various ships; not all are recorded but his name appears on

the New York Passenger Lists for the *Adriatic* arriving from Liverpool in May, June and July 1931, and on one of the last voyages of her sister ship the *Baltic* in January 1932. (When launched in 1903, the *Baltic* was the largest ship in the world, notable for having relayed an iceberg warning to the *Titanic* and being in radio contact with her during the sinking, though 300 miles away. The *Baltic* was scrapped in February 1933.)

Beryl left school at the end of 1928 having gained her Senior School Certificate in eight subjects. Her headmaster gave her a good reference:

The County School,
Llandysul.
Sept 18 1928.

<u>*To whom it may concern:*</u>

I have much pleasure in recommending Beryl Parkington. After four years' tuition she gained a particularly brilliant School Certificate of the Central Welsh Board, qualifying at the same time for Matriculation.

The high general excellence of her attainments would warrant her entering any profession but her ambition is to succeed in a commercial career.

Her powers of application are remarkable and her comprehension quick and sound.

She has a pleasing and obliging disposition and was very popular with Staff and pupils.

Having regard to her talents and her industry I have no hesitation in saying that she will prove highly successful in whatever branch of business she may have the opportunity to serve.

JE Parry
Headmaster.

Beryl completed a course in Pitman's Shorthand whilst working as a secretary for her father, and achieved a speed of 120 words per minute in an exam at the Pitman's Phonetics Institute in Bath on May 14, 1930.

There was work available in London, and she accepted employment as a shorthand typist with the Amalgamated

Dental Company Ltd in Piccadilly from 1930 to 1932. She boarded with Annie's brother Willie and family in Islington, travelling to work by bus and tube train.

Annie, like Rachel, was a caring mother, and helped Beryl in small ways when she could.

<u>Annie to Beryl.</u>
Electra House,
Newcastle-Emlyn.
Oct 18 1930.

My dear Beryl,

This is to wish you Very Many Happy Returns of the Day. May you always have a happy and good life, if not rich.

I meant to have bought you a real leather handbag, but as you prefer having the money I am enclosing some towards your winter coat. If you were living in Newcastle-Emlyn you would have had to get one before now. It's been terrible here – wind, rain and cold.

Am also sending under separate cover your old navy costume made up. Now don't think it's not good enough, dear – it looks lovely and the stuff is gents' suiting. It will always look good and be warm for winter days. If you prefer you could change the collar and cuffs for fancy ones.

Also find enclosed a few Welsh Cakes. I would have made you a big cake, dear, but I thought it too soon after the other one.

With fondest love from us to you, dear daughter, on your 19th birthday.

Mother and Dad XXX

Early Letters

While on the Liverpool - New York run, Leonard had been able to take short breaks between voyages, and to visit his parents at Llandrindod Wells. He was home at the end of 1931, but was to be transferred from the *Baltic* to the *Silvercypress* in New York on the next voyage. This was a passenger-cargo vessel which ran round the world via the Panama and Suez Canals without visiting Britain. It meant that he might be away for several years before seeing his family again.

In 1932 he renewed his friendship with Beryl. He started writing to her, and she wrote back. Letters were the only general means of communication in those days (telegrams were prohibitively expensive) but took weeks to arrive in other countries as they usually had to travel by sea; replies were equally slow. Air mail was in its infancy, only available to some destinations, and expensive.

The *Silvercypress* offered new sights and experiences, including the immediate aftermath of the Sino-Japanese battle at Shanghai, known as the *January 28 incident*, which Leonard shared with Beryl:

<u>Leonard to Beryl.</u>   *m/v Silvercypress,*
en route Merka to Genoa.
May 8 1932.

Dear Beryl,
Usually I spend this part of the afternoon stretched out in my bunk with a book in my hands, apparently reading, but more than likely lost in the land of dreams. However this afternoon I have an important engagement with the

"Llandovery Castle" in two hours time, and fearing that I'd just drop off to sleep again, I thought I'd write this letter instead.

Life with me nowadays seems quite comfortable. I was transferred in New York from the White Star Liner "Baltic" in January last, and am now in charge of a beautiful 10,000 tons motor vessel that carries a few dozen passengers, and runs round the world.

Photo: www.shipsnostalgia.com

The *Silvercypress.*

Up to the time of writing the trip has been a very pleasant one. Leaving New York on January 30 we took a southward course, and averaging a steady 16½ knots arrived in Colon, the entrance to the Panama Canal, 10 days later. No ships are allowed through the canal during the hours of darkness, so we anchored here for the night and left again at six next morning.

Entering the canal we steamed for about two miles up what appeared to be a wide river. On either side the banks were covered with thick tropical undergrowth. Occasionally I heard the call of love birds, and looking forward saw a range of low mountains. I was just wondering how on earth we would climb over these when a bend in the canal brought us in full view of the locks and a solution to my problem.

There are three locks in all on the Atlantic side of the canal, each of which lifted us a height of fifty feet. The whole process took about an hour, after which we entered a huge lake, very wide to start, but later narrowing into a channel barely wide enough for two ships to pass, and after journeying along this for six hours we arrived at the Pacific end, where four more locks dropped us into the Pacific Ocean bound for San Pedro, a small port midway along the coast of "Sunny California".

We arrived in San Pedro on February 22, and here I spent the nicest three days of my life. Some kind stevedore placed two of his cars at the disposal of the ship's officers. The first day we made a tour of Hollywood and Beverley Hills visiting the Fox, Paramount and Harold Lloyd film studios, where we got a brief insight of a few of the tricks of picture making. The next day was spent touring Los Angeles, seeing colourful fiestas, old Spanish missions, and harbours with ships from the seven seas; and the last day we spent in San Pedro itself, finishing up with a quiet walk through palm-lined boulevards and along the coast, where foaming breakers invited a cool plunge.

Alas, all good things must come to an end, and on February 25 we left San Pedro and taking a westward course, commenced our crossing of the Pacific Ocean, bound for Yokohama and Kobe, Japan. Weather conditions up to now had been ideal and continued so for the next few days. We hardly ever had any rain, days were comfortably free from humidity, while nights were cool enough to enjoy sleeping under blankets. As we got a little further north, however, conditions became very much worse.

The first intimation we got of approaching bad weather was heavy rain and bad snow squalls, which later became so persistent that the ship's speed had to be reduced by half, owing to bad visibility. Worse was to come, however, and about five days before reaching Yokohama we encountered a real Pacific storm. Heavy seas started pitching us all over the place. One minute we were high up on the crest of a wave, so high that we could almost see Asia and America at the same time, and then with a splash we'd go crashing down into a hollow again. The rough seas would sweep over the decks, lifting the lifeboats from their moorings, and carrying anything that wasn't securely lashed down overboard. We had two solid days of this weather; in fact, things were so bad at one time that a passing ship wanted to know who we were and called: "Two masts, one funnel, who are you?"

Owing to this bad weather we were three days late arriving in Yokohama, as a result of which our stay was only a short one. Silks are the main attraction here, and most of us procured wardrobes of silk goods fit for the Prince of Wales, and at a price that compares more than favourably with cotton goods at home.

Anyway, our lightning call at Yokohama was followed by an equally quick one in Kobe, and after business was completed here we set out for Shanghai, arriving at the mouth of the river four days later on March 19.

You probably know the history of the war that has been going on here, but God! what a mess the place was in. The forts at the mouth of the river could not be seen for wreckage, and later up the river the village of Woosung was shot to blazes, people were moving about the wreckage trying to recover their belongings, while blazing fires scattered around indicated gangs of workers collecting dead bodies and burning them. The only places that had not been hit at all were houses scattered here and there flying either the British or American flags.

What a difference, though, when we arrived in the International Settlement: business went on as usual, houses were all intact and, except for the fact that a few regiments of Japanese soldiers paraded the streets, and that curfew had been declared at 11 pm, one would never dream that only a fortnight before, a fierce battle had raged only a mile or two away. Still, this was only to be expected really, as Japan fought China, not Europe; but the strange part is that although there has been all this fighting, neither side has declared war!

Anyway, we stayed in Shanghai a week, but as we were confined entirely to the Settlement, I didn't relish the idea of going ashore much, except to a cabaret or dance, and spent most of my time instead overhauling batteries and testing little gadgets of my own idea, which proved to be only gadgets after all.

We left Shanghai on March 26, and since then have been in and out of ports almost daily, visiting the Philippine Islands, Dutch East Indies, Straits Settlements, India and Ceylon, and finally Merka in Italian Somaliland; and now we're about half way through the Red Sea.

The weather during the latter part of our voyage was beautiful, and compared favourably with that described along the American coast. The last two days however have been terribly hot: yesterday it was 115° in the shade, and today it reached 120°. However, we expect to reach Suez tomorrow night and Port Said in two and a half days, after which the Mediterranean I hope will prove much cooler.

Our only other port of call then, before returning to New York, will be Genoa. We do not touch Britain at all and I expect it will be two or three years before I get a glimpse of the old country again, however I'm awfully comfortable here. I enjoy the run and life on the whole is wonderful, so I have no reason to grumble.

If you do feel like answering this letter I think the best address will be:

> *wo/c Silvercypress*
> *c/o British Wireless Marine Service*
> *40 Rector Street*
> *New York City*
> *USA*

By writing there I am always assured of receiving letters, for in the event of my being transferred to another ship, they'll know where to send them whereas others probably would not.

We expect to arrive in New York around May 30, and unless I get transferred to some other ship, will have a month's holiday there, and we're due to commence another world voyage on June 27.

If it is possible, however, I should very much like to be transferred to a ship bound for South America or Australia, as these are the only continents I have not visited now.

I'm afraid I've been long-winded with this account of my adventures; if I have, I'm sorry, and as there's only 20 minutes to go before I keep my appointment with the "Llandovery Castle" I think I'll close and go out on deck for a breather, though it makes no difference really where I go – it's stifling hot anywhere around here.

> *Cofion gorau,*
> *Leonard.*

Just after Leonard posted this letter to Beryl from Suez, something very sad and unexpected occurred. His mother Rachel, whom he adored, died aged 56 of "galloping consumption" (miliary tuberculosis) in Llandrindod Wells on May 10 1932.

A telegram awaited him with the news at Port Said. Separated by oceans from his family, there was no way to share his grief with them except by letter, but he cabled back *Take care of Raymond* and wrote of his distress to Maggie. She sent a long, gentle reply:

<u>Maggie to Leonard.</u>

The Rock Hotel,
Llandysul.
June 15 1932.

My dear Leonard,

We were ever so pleased to get your letter on Monday. I felt I couldn't write the awful news to you until we had a letter, but I'm sorry now, for if I had written there and then, you'd know all about it by this time.

I'm very glad you are sticking at it, as we'd much rather you finish your foreign service first, and I know Mam would also wish it, for she was always looking forward to the end of that. I hope, Leonard bach, that by now you are feeling better over it than when you wrote. You must not be unhappy or broken hearted, Leonard boy, because we might be making it harder for her by being so.

No dear, I'm sorry to say she did not leave a message or say "goodbye" to any of us. You see, she carried her illness on her feet and really did not know she was ill: it was only from the Friday to the Tuesday evening the 10th of May. She cooked the breakfast for Dad and Raymond on Friday morning as usual, and told Dad she was going to have a sit down that morning as she was feeling a little tired, and told him to take the key of the door with him as she wasn't going to answer anyone. He'd done that heaps of times before and didn't think anything of it.

Well, when he came home dinner time, he found everything as he'd left it that morning, but the fire was clean out. So he went upstairs to look for Mam, and found her in bed with her clothes on and slightly delirious.

He got the doctor, and he said to get someone to look after her. Gertie went at once on Saturday morning. I went up myself on the Sunday as Dad told you, and stayed until we brought her back the following Saturday to Carmel cemetery. I am sure it will comfort you to know that everything possible was done for her. Mr Swete said he'd pay for a specialist or anything else that could save her. But she was beyond all human aid. God wanted her back, so he took her very mercifully. She felt no pain at all, only weakness – she told me so heaps of times. The doctor said so, too. She seemed to be quite at ease, nothing troubled her – in fact, she seemed to forget all about this world altogether.

She seemed to be quite satisfied with everything and everybody. She thought I was just up there for the weekend and she said "Leonard will be in Liverpool tomorrow, you see, and will come home then on Tuesday, and you'll see him before you go back," and she seemed so pleased with that. That was about the last thing she said about us children. After that, she spoke very lovingly of how good Dad had always been, and something about him deserving a good home. She was all mixed up like that till Tuesday morning. She didn't know him on Tuesday, and thought at times that I was Gertie. She never once mentioned anything about dying or seeing anyone, and never bothered at all even about Raymond. She didn't seem to remember about him or anyone else after Monday. I know that if you were here and could see her, you'd have been quite willing dear for her sake, as you'd never be so selfish as to wish her to linger in that state. She was lovely to nurse to the very end, and she wanted for nothing that this world could give her.

The last words she spoke were: "What does the psalm say?

– 'Thus saith the Lord.'" After that, she dropped into unconsciousness and never recovered. She died as she had always wished it: she always said she hoped she would go from the middle of her work, and be unconscious at the end, and have a very short illness.

Of course, the world seems to be quite a different place since she's gone, but for her sake we must carry on, and I hope you'll be brave. I know it's very hard for you out there all alone, but you have our prayers and the sympathy of all Llandysul and those who knew us at Llandrindod. We had a little service at Rock Cottage before we left Llandrindod on the Saturday morning, then had the proper service in our church here at Llandysul, and took her up to Carmel cemetery. She rests beside Uncle Isaac by the trees. She had a very large funeral and I feel that she looked on the scene with approval, from above.

We miss her terribly every day of our lives and will always do so, but she'll be waiting for us now when our time comes, and it will not be so hard to bear, knowing she's there to greet us, so we must strive to live a good life and follow her example so that we can make sure of that meeting.

Raymond and Gertie are really wonderful. We all try to help and comfort each other as best we can, dear. God has helped us to bear up and I know he'll help you too, for if he sends his trials, he also gives us strength to bear them.

We've had some very nice letters from friends, and I shall keep them all for you to see when you return, or I'll send them on, if you like – you let me know. We have also taken a photo of the grave from three angles for you.

Gertie is going to look after Dad now, and Raymond is

home with me. I shall try to get him something to do here or in Carmarthen, so I can look after him. Gertie and Dad are going to move into a little flat in Llandrindod – Arianwen flats, up by the School. I shall go up next Tuesday to put things right there, and then Gertie will go up. She doesn't want to go back to the cottage at all; she'd rather carry on here while I go and get everything out of there. I wish we could afford for Dad to come back here now, but you see, there's nothing here and he earns good money up there, but as soon as we can afford it, they'll both come home for good. Dad is very cut up – he misses her most of all and I feel really sorry for him. I know Gertie will be good to him and do all she can for him.

I hope you'll be a good boy, Leonard, and write and come home as often as you can. I hope Mam's not being here will not make any difference that way. I will always do my very best for all of you, but I can never fill her place. I will write again next week, so cheerio. All our love dear boy, and be brave.

> *Your loving sister,*
> *Maggie XXX*

<u>Beryl to Leonard.</u>

> *c/o 11 Barnsbury Square,*
> *London N1.*
> *July 27 1932.*

Dear Leonard,

Winnie Evans wrote to tell me the sad news about your Mam. It must have been a terrible shock for all your family, but especially you, being so far away. Please accept my deepest sympathy in your awful loss - I suppose losing one's parents is something we all have to face one day, but not what we anticipate at our age. I've written a little note of sympathy to Gertie.

Thank you for your nice interesting letter posted in Suez. My goodness, what an adventurous life you lead! It's a far cry from the days when we were at the "Ysgol ar y Bryn" together, isn't it? I remember Mr Hughes teaching us in Geography about a lot of the places you mention – now you know they're actually there!

You didn't mention if you were sea sick in those heavy seas in the North Pacific - I'm sure I would have been. The war zone around Shanghai sounds horrible. I did read something about it in the newspaper but never imagined you would have been there.

Well, my life in London is much less exciting than yours. I'm staying with my Uncle Willie and his family – Aunty Dolly, and cousins David (10) and Adeline (4). They are kindness itself. Uncle Willie's very fatherly – he's a lot older than Aunty Dolly, but she absolutely dotes on him. He works as a draper at Whiteley's Department Store. He's been there for years, but I don't think he earns very much and the board I pay gives them a bit more income.

Aunty Dolly's a real Londoner with a great sense of humour. For some reason she calls Uncle Willie "Horace", which she pronounces as "'Orris". The house has three storeys, and I get the giggles when she's on the top floor and she shouts "'Orris!" to him in the basement!

David and Adeline are quiet children. They love me reading stories to them, and we often go to play in the park over the road. Adeline's just started at the same school as

David. It's not far away; they walk there together and he holds her hand tightly all the way there and back.

I must tell you about Jim, the cat. He's a black and white stray that Aunty took pity on and fed one day. Of course he immediately took up residence here and has lived with them for about four years! Despite his battle-worn appearance, he is the most affable old thing. He jumps into my lap as soon as I sit down, and purrs his heart out. If I ignore him I get a gentle nip as a reminder that he's there!

I've been working as a secretary at the Amalgamated Dental Company in Piccadilly for over two years now. They make all sorts of weird and wonderful dentists' equipment and supplies at their factory in Walton on Thames but we handle all the orders and correspondence. My shorthand and typing are improving all the time with practice – I expect you find the same with Morse code. (Someone was telling me the other day that Wireless Operators can tell who's sending a message from the way they key the dots and dashes. I find that amazing!) Isn't it a coincidence how we both use codes in our work: you Morse, me shorthand.

The weather has been very warm lately. London's a bit airless in the summer, though nothing like as stifling as you experienced in Suez. It would be nice to be able to visit Aberporth or Tresaith and get some sea air.

When I was little, we used to go with Grandpa and Granny, taking a pony and trap. We might as well have walked all the way – half the journey was uphill and we had to spare the pony, then on the way down he was slipping and we had to walk again! They used to rent a cottage almost on the beach at Aberporth for a month, and a lot of the family used to come and stay at different times.

Still, I've got a good job here with nice accommodation, and I'm very thankful for that in these difficult times, when so many people are unemployed all over the country.

Tom took his CWB Senior exam last month and we're expecting the results soon. Mother is rather concerned as she didn't think he was studying nearly hard enough, but we'll see!

I've been to the cinema a couple of times lately and seen two good films: a thriller called "The Frightened Lady" starring our own Emlyn Williams, and a comedy with Leslie Howard, "Service For Ladies". Uncle Willie doesn't like me going to the cinema; he's very religious and thinks it's sinful, so to make up for it I took him along last Sunday evening to the Welsh chapel in Holloway where we sang hymns at the tops of our voices!

Well, I hope you're keeping well and that this letter reaches you, wherever you are!

> *Best wishes,*
> *Beryl.*

Leonard's second trip round the world from New York was cut short in Singapore, where he was transferred to the *Hong Kheng*, a passenger ship belonging to the Straits Steamship Line and plying between Rangoon, Singapore and Hong Kong.

Leonard to Beryl.

s/s Hong Kheng,
Singapore.
September 13 1932.

Dear Beryl,

Thanks ever so much for your letter received in Batavia on September 2. After the many letters of sympathy I have received of late, it was a welcome change, and I enjoyed reading it immensely.

I am no longer in charge of the "Silvercypress", but am now second operator on this ship. I have not in any way been demoted, as the "Silvercypress" is under 12,000 tons and therefore only a Class II ship, whereas this ship is 16,000 tons and has three operators, besides which I get an increase in pay of 18/- per month, owing to the extra tonnage. We carry about 3,000 passengers and are on a regular run from Rangoon to Singapore and Hong Kong.

The "Silvercypress" left last night and as she passed us in the harbour gave me a lovely farewell, sending "Goodbye and Good Luck" on the Morse lamp, and then blowing three blasts on the siren. I was naturally a little thrilled, and a faint shiver ran down my spine as she disappeared in the distance, for after all she had been my home, and a very happy one, for nearly nine months.

Rather an amusing incident occurred in Batavia. We arrived there at 8 am on August 31. As our bows crossed the harbour entrance a Dutch warship let off a salute of 21 guns, and as the echo of the last shot died in the distance, every ship in the harbour became adorned with flags. We were very thrilled at receiving such a welcome, for naturally we thought it was for us. We could not make the ship curtsey in response, - it's just as well we couldn't, for later we learned that August 31 is the Dutch Queen's birthday. The salute and flags were in her honour, and our arrival had not even been noticed!

Photo: www.wrecksite.eu

The *Hong Kheng.*

Pardon me if I make any bad mistakes tonight, as I am not yet fully recovered from a nasty bump I had this afternoon. The chief operator, the second mate and I went out in the lifeboat, and as there was a good breeze blowing, decided to hoist the sails. Everything went well for about an hour, when suddenly a cross current of air sent the boom over to the other side. I must have been in the way, for all I remember was a terrific whack across the back of my head, and the next minute I was in the water. Fortunately there were no sharks around at the time, and I suffered no more severe damage than a good wetting and a slight headache!

Since joining this ship I have had plenty to keep me busy. Every morning we go for a run in the doctor's car (he lives here) and this morning went to Johore, a small town about 15 miles away. On our way we drove through huge rubber plantations, stopped at one of the factories, and saw how rubber is treated from the time it leaves the trees in liquid form, to the time it is packed for export. We visited the Sultan of Johore's palace and then went to the temple and saw the Holy Carpets.

In the afternoons we usually go out in the lifeboat. There is a lovely bathing pool about five miles from here, where we swim before returning to the ship for dinner. In the evenings we often have a great singsong on the boat deck.

I don't know how long I shall be on this ship, as she is in need of engine repairs and may have to dry dock. However as long as she runs, we'll be calling in Singapore about every 10 days, so for the present my address will be:

> *c/o British Wireless Marine Service Co.*
> *Hong Kong Bank Chambers*
> *Collier's Quay*
> *Singapore.*

I shall of course welcome any letters if you can still spare the time, and in the event of my being transferred, they will forward them from the office to wherever I am.

I think I've told you all the news. Let me know how Tom got on in CWB and give him my "Cofion Gorau".

Hoping that you and all at home are enjoying good health, and with my kindest regards and best wishes,

> *Yours very sincerely,*
> *Leonard.*

Torpedoed Dreams

The South China Sea was then (and still is) the haunt of pirates. The Straits Steamship Line had the bridges and engine rooms of its ships protected by grilles, the ships carried revolvers and shotguns for use by the Officers and Engineers, also armed guards patrolled the thousand or so deck passengers. Pre-arranged signals could be sent by the ships to the British Naval Authorities in Hong Kong and if that wasn't enough to deter would-be pirates, the Officers regularly had target practice when on passage, just to let it be known to all on board that the ship's staff were armed.

<u>Leonard to Beryl.</u>

s/s Hong Kheng,
Penang.
November 15 1932.

Dear Beryl,

One of the most pleasant pastimes in the tropics is that of sun bathing. Like everything else however, it has its limits, and if one stays out in the sun too long, he is apt to become uncomfortably hot. For that reason, therefore, I have had to retire into the shade in order to write this letter.

After a period of nearly two months I have now completed my first voyage on this ship. In my last letter I described the trip from Singapore to Hong Kong, then from there we went to Swatow and Amoy and back again to Hong Kong, where we went into dry dock for a month.

Whatever people have against serving their foreign service on the China coast, I like it very much myself. The run from Hong Kong to Amoy is particularly beautiful. We hug the coast most of the way, and pass between numerous small islands; indeed, so numerous are they, that one has the impression of sailing along a long winding river, whose banks are very rugged and rocky, and rise steeply almost from the water's edge.

Hong Kong, Amoy and Swatow have nothing particularly interesting to offer tourists (in the way of novelties, I mean) and during our stay in those places, our daily pleasures consisted of occasional games of tennis and cricket, plenty of swimming, a few dances, and visits to the theatre or pictures.

After our stay in Hong Kong we returned to Singapore and then went to Rangoon, which is situated on the river Irrawaddy, about 30 miles from the mouth. We stayed here for five days and during that week, the mission was particularly active.

On the first night of our arrival I went to a whist drive organised by them, and succeeded in carrying off the gents' second prize with a score of 180 for 22 hands. The second night they organised a moonlight bathing party; there were about 115 of us there, made up of about 70 men and 45 ladies. We left the mission in four huge charabancs and drove out to the lakes about 7 miles away, and after our bathing we had a huge supper party and ended the evening with dancing on the green.

The other three nights we were there they had a big dance, which owing to the heat was not a great success; another whist drive in which I played very badly; and finally a concert given by the orchestra of the P&O Liner "Rajaputra". The following morning we left Rangoon on our return voyage to Hong Kong, arriving here this morning and due to leave sometime tomorrow.

From what I've told you of the run you'll gather that there is not a great deal of excitement attached to it. However, one cannot always be seeking thrills, and there are plenty of thrills on board here without seeking them elsewhere.

To begin with, you probably read an account of the recent piracies on this coast. First of all that of the "Helicon", and

Leonard on the *Hong Kheng* in 1932, aged 21.

then the "Hong Hwa" (which by the way is our sister ship.) In the past three years the authorities have managed pretty well to keep down the pirates, but of late they have become fairly active again and our own ship is just as liable to be pirated as any other, although we could give them a pretty rough time if they came.

All these ships out here carry a number of Chinese as deck passengers. Our own quarters are on the boat deck, and we are guarded from the rest of the ship in that there is only one approach to us, and this is barred off with iron grilles over which two armed guards keep watch night and day. Along the ship's side, between the passenger deck and our own, is a network of barbed wire, so that if any pirates come aboard as deck passengers (as is always the case), they have either to overpower the guards or climb the barbed wire, neither of which of course is impossible.

Anyway, to continue about our thrilling episodes: we were passing Bias Bay – the headquarters of the pirates – one afternoon when there was a terrible commotion below.

Fearing that we were really being pirated, we all armed ourselves with two revolvers and 50 rounds of ammunition each, and when the Captain strode through the iron gate we all kept our eyes open ready to shoot the first man that attacked him. Suddenly we saw him throw down his revolvers, and take a small rubber club out of his pocket and aim it at someone. We couldn't see what had happened owing to the crowd, but he was evidently satisfied and motioned us forward, and there lying at his feet was the body of an unconscious Chinese man. In his right hand he grasped a large pointed dagger, and his clothes were a mass of blood.

Torpedoed Dreams

To cut a long story short the poor fellow had gone mad, and run amongst the passengers stabbing at anyone who came his way. Fortunately no-one was killed, though four passengers were very severely injured.

On another occasion I was on watch in the wireless room one night when I saw a man climbing the barbed wire fence. I have never aimed a gun at any man before, so you can excuse the cold shiver that ran down my spine as I carefully aimed my revolver at this man – our orders are to shoot on sight, and no misses, and I was determined that on this occasion there would be no miss!

However, I was spared the agony myself, for just as I was going to fire, two shots rang out simultaneously from the bridge, and the man disappeared. We found him a little later lying on the deck below. One bullet had hit him in the thigh, and another in the arm, but otherwise he was unhurt and on questioning him it appeared that the poor fellow had found it rather stuffy below and was merely trying to get on the boat deck for some fresh air!

However, we all think his real reason will always be a mystery. He may have been telling the truth, although there were plenty of places he could go for fresh air without climbing barbed wire! On the other hand, goodness knows what would have happened had he succeeded, and perhaps our act in shooting him down was not a callous one in that it scared away any accomplices he might have had.

Unfortunately I can't supply newspaper cuttings in proof of the adventures I have told you about. Every effort is made to hush up these things, as they affect our trade badly if any news leaks out; however I enclose a cutting about the piracy of the "Helicon" that might prove interesting.

Hoping all are well at home and that Tom was successful in his CWB examinations,

Yours very sincerely,
Leonard.

Leonard to Beryl.

s/s Hong Kheng,
At Sea.
December 13 1932.

Dear Beryl,

We are due in Singapore on Dec 15 and I should simply hate the idea of another letter waiting me there before I have first replied to those received on Nov 19. Please excuse my not writing sooner but honestly, it wasn't worth while. Had I written at any time during our previous visit to South China, the letter would merely have returned to Singapore on this ship, so I thought that by delaying a little longer I might pick up something really interesting to write about.

South China at this time of the year is not a place that poets would sing about. With all due respect to the dignity of Hong Kong, and the rarefied air of its Victoria Peak, the place as a whole has an unhealthy atmosphere. Its breath is that of the drying room of a Chinese laundry; overnight one's shoes accumulate a covering of green mould, and one wakes in the morning with a feeling that a cross section of the lungs would resemble a slice of Gorgonzola cheese! The weather too was comparatively cold, and perhaps the only time I really enjoyed myself was when I was asleep in my bunk, well tucked in under four blankets!

Life among the Chinese however seemed not in the least

bit affected by the adverse climatic conditions. Already preparations were being made for an anticipated boom in trade during Xmas. In the main streets of Hong Kong one could gaze at window displays that were worthy of Selfridges or any other large London stores, while in the smaller and narrower side streets, Chinese shopkeepers were no less enterprising, and quaint advertisements written on flags in Chinese symbols told the world of the particular bargains they had to offer.

I haven't told you anything of street scenes in China. The contrasts are many and there is a variety of traffic here that surely exists only in the East. Apart from the more modern forms of transport – motor vehicles, electric trams and traction engines – one can also see wheelbarrows that trundle along with tremendous loads, coolies turned beasts of burden bearing bales and baskets of tremendous weight; two wheeled carts sometimes drawn by oxen, but more often utilising human power, with perhaps six or eight perspiring coolies at the shafts. In addition there are rickshaws, which are now well past their usefulness as a means of transport, and occasionally when wishing to reach some destination unapproachable by other means, one may be able to procure a "Sedan Chair" of a type that is slung on two long poles, and is carried by a couple of coolies.

Night life is a mixture of the old world and the new. Along narrow pavements or at street corners, one can find large crowds assembled to discuss the events of the day. In front of one of the large hotels, a bright coloured limousine unloads a group of people to attend a formal dinner, others may be attending theatres or cinemas or the more wealthy

Chinese restaurants. At modern night clubs and cabarets, jazz bands may be belching forth a rhythmic melody, while perhaps outside a lone hawker pipes a few wavering notes on his flageolet, hoping for one more customer to buy his pickled fruits before retiring wearily for the night.

Turning from the streets to the waterways, one can also observe ceaseless activity. Nearly fifty million tons of foreign shipping visit Chinese ports in a year. Hundreds of junks move up and down with the tides. Some of them are very large and heavy, with high colourfully-painted sterns (to ward off devils) and engaged in transport work up and down the coast. Others of a much smaller size are engaged in fishing, or carrying of cargo between the lesser distanced places. Out in the bays huge ocean liners lie at anchor; all around them but of no less importance are freighters, oil tankers, and colliers; and flitting here and there, managed with a skill that is amazing, one finds the smaller traffic: launches, flat-bottomed boats, and sampans.

When discussing slavery today one usually associates it with the past, but surely there is no other way of describing the lives of the lower class Chinese. It is a life of hardship and poverty. In my previous remarks re coolie power, one has ample evidence of these hardships: the wages they receive for a month's work only amounts to five or six shillings. Gazing out to sea, one can see a familiar sight: dotted here and there over the water are the flat bottomed boats and sampans. A couple of women may be standing in the stern, battling against a strong tide and operating heavy two-handed oars with a forward pushing movement. In the bows sitting down, but striving none the less hard, one may see two very small children; the skill they show in handling heavy oars is amazing. European children of the same age or even older could not even lift them from the ground, let alone carry out the actual operation of rowing!

However, in spite of all the hardships the people as a whole appear to be quite happy and enjoy life to the full. I have written rather a lot about the Chinese in my letters, but you must remember that every hour of my life at present is spent among them. In Singapore and Penang, the Chinese population far exceeds that of any other race; and regarding Rangoon, I have only been there once, and will write about life in that part when I have become a little more accustomed to it.

For the time being, however, my pen is becoming rather heated: if I don't stop writing soon I fear it will scorch the paper, and that would be a catastrophe – I couldn't address the envelope then!

Anyway, I hope all at home are enjoying good health, that Tom enjoyed his cycling holiday, and that by now you are quite well and fit again.

Cheerio and Cofion Gorau.
Yours very truly,
Leonard.

<u>Leonard to Beryl.</u>   *s/s Hong Kheng,*
Singapore.
30 December 1932.

Dear Beryl,
Thanks very much for all your letters received here today; dear me, I don't know whether I ought to write a lot of

letters in reply, or what to do! I'm lagging behind badly, but at any rate, they amused me terribly. I haven't yet stopped laughing over the bandit incident, while the Xmas card was the essence of cheerfulness.

I quite enjoyed our visit to Rangoon this time. The place itself is not particularly interesting, neither is the scenery very beautiful, but I saw quite a few things that were interesting enough to overcome these disadvantages.

First on the list comes the Shwedagon Pagoda. This is a magnificent temple, and in appearance resembles St Paul's Cathedral. During the day its huge golden dome reflects the rays of the sun to such extent that it looks like a ball of fire, while at night the building is lit by nearly a thousand electric lamps, and can be seen from miles away.

Before we could enter we had to take off our shoes, and once inside we saw beautiful images of animals carved in stone. On a high altar facing the east were three priests dressed in very bright yellow loin cloths, and known as "Canaries". A never-ending throng of natives entered and left the place, bringing gifts of all kinds, and depositing them in bowls at their feet.

After the Pagoda we visited some of the rice fields. Rice is one of Burma's chief products. The country, which is very flat along the banks of the River Irrawaddy, is particularly adaptable for this purpose, and we spent hours watching coolies up to their knees in water, transplanting rice stalks. The plants are first cultivated in nurseries, then when the rainy season floods the land, they are dug up and replanted in the rice fields. Each stalk is planted separately, in squares four to six inches apart.

Torpedoed Dreams

Another scene that interested me greatly was that of elephants at work. These are engaged mostly in the timber industry, and during a conversation with one of the European foremen, I gathered quite a lot of information about it.

Teak is the hardest wood available. It is grown up in the hilly districts of Burma, and there are many dangers that the men face whilst engaged in timbering it. Timbering is usually carried out during the dry season. Elephants are used for hauling, and for clearing away thick undergrowth. When the trees have been cut down, the logs are gathered along the hillsides and deep channels are cut from them to the river. During the rainy season these logs are washed down by the torrential rains, and all along the river men gather them into rafts and float them down to the sawmills, where they are left until the wood is properly seasoned.

When they are ready for trimming they are moved again to the mills. Elephants are used, and their intelligence is marvellous. At a word from their drivers they grip a log at one end with their trunks and drag it to the required position. Sometimes they come across logs that are too heavy for one animal, and more are used, and it is here that one really marvels at their training. Every action seems to be timed. At a word they grip the log together, and carry it step by step to where it is wanted. A false move is hardly ever made, and they won't budge an inch until each has a firm grip with its trunk.

Christmas day was spent at sea again this year. There isn't much to describe really, as personally I could see no difference to other Christmases, except of course that I was away from home and had to keep my watches just the same.

I enclose a menu of our Xmas dinner which I managed to grab, and after dinner we had the usual games and dancing. Altogether it was a jolly day and I quite enjoyed myself, turning in at 10 pm though, as I had to be on watch again at midnight.

I shan't be at all surprised if I'm sent home very shortly. From the first of January, the Company are introducing a new economy scheme, which means that...   (Remainder missing).

Trade in and around Singapore was still suffering after the Depression, also the Straits Steamship Line was facing increasing competition. However its chairman, CE Wurtzburg, was able to keep its profits rising after a slight dip in 1933.

Leonard to Beryl.   *s/s Hong Kheng,*
Penang.
January 24 1933.

Dear Beryl
Thanks very much for your long interesting letter received in Singapore yesterday. At first it puzzled me terribly, being registered. I was fully prepared to find a cheque for at least a thousand pounds enclosed, however the fact that the cheque was missing didn't decrease the value, as it was the only letter I received yesterday, and one feels so disappointed when others receive letters and they themselves don't!

This business of my changing ships has rather upset the smooth running of my correspondence. The fault is due to the operator who relieved me on the "Silvercypress" having kept all the letters until they arrived in New York before readdressing them to me. I don't know how many letters you have written, but I have now received seven letters since the Batavia one, and as the "Silvercypress" left Singapore about four days ago, I should think I have received them all now.

I haven't anything thrilling to describe to you this time, unless you would call suicides thrilling. Seven men threw themselves overboard during our voyage from Hong Kong to Amoy, but these things happen so frequently that we don't even stop to pick them up now.

It is rather hard to understand the mentality of some Chinese, but as far as these suicides are concerned, the person committing suicide thoroughly believes that the water god has called him. He frantically resists any attempt made to save him, and even if he is saved, he just jumps overboard again at the next opportunity, believing that only bad luck can come to him during his life on earth if the water god is robbed of his prey.

The weather up north was very bad this time, again. In Hong Kong it was wet and miserable, and the only form of entertainment we engaged in was a visit to the cinema. We saw two films, Buster Keaton in "The Passionate Plumber", and an English musical production "Good Night Vienna". The former was the usual amusing antics of the actor who never smiles, but I particularly enjoyed the latter, and the theme song "Good Night Vienna", when played as a tango, is a particularly lilting melody.

Talking of music, you seem to be doing very well lately, although I'm sure Tom is an awful tease. Anyway, even if what he accuses you of was correct, well, you showed more common sense than he would have done, and you are still responsible for them winning the first prize!

Time seems to be passing very slowly lately, and I feel terribly excited over the prospect of coming home shortly. I was definitely told in Singapore yesterday that my days out here are numbered now, but that in all probability, owing to the fact that others have to be transferred first, I won't be transferred much before April or May. Anyway, I haven't very long to wait now, and the delay is all for the best. I should find the climate of Wales a bit unsatisfactory just now, but given decent summer weather it will be very pleasant.

Hoping you are still enjoying improved health, and that Tom's teasing doesn't worry you unduly.

Yours very sincerely,
Leonard.

<u>Leonard to Beryl.</u>

P&O RMS Chitral,
Singapore.
April 27 1933.

Dear Beryl,
Thanks very much for your letter of February 21 received here yesterday. I've been trying to post you one for weeks now, but owing to this beastly Sino-Japanese war, letters are taking from twelve to fifteen weeks to be delivered in Britain from China and Japan, so I thought the best thing to do was to wait and post via Air Mail from here.

You see, I was transferred from the "Hong Kheng" in Singapore here on March 18. Since then I've been to Shanghai, Kobe (Japan) and Yokohama. Time does not permit of my writing a detailed account of my adventures in these places as we're leaving here in an hour for Penang, after which we visit Colombo, Aden, Port Said, Malta, Marseilles, Gibraltar, and London, being due in London on May 26. However there are three whole weeks to go between now and our arrival in Marseilles, so during that time I will endeavour to write as interesting an account as possible of my experiences to date, and also between now and our arrival in Marseilles. Meanwhile, if you feel like writing to Marseilles my address there will be:

> *Wireless Dept RMS Chitral*
> *c/o P&O Agents Messrs Estrine & Co.*
> *18 Rue Colbert*
> *Marseilles.*

You know I always appreciate letters no matter how short they are, but as you have to post from Britain not later than May 15 I doubt very much whether you'll have the time.

Anyway, it's very gratifying to know that I am now homeward bound; the thought cheers me up wonderfully, and I'm looking forward very much to the long spell of leave (three months, I believe) that is at the end of this voyage.

Forgive this hasty scrawl and please accept my kindest regards and best wishes.

> *Yours very sincerely,*
> *Len.*

Beryl had returned to Newcastle-Emlyn and was working as a clerk for D. Roy Evans, a local solicitor. Her typing skills had improved in London, and she could work accurately at a good speed; essential with legal documents where no corrections could be made on the typewriters then in use. On one occasion she had to attend a murder trial and was very apprehensive that she would have to view the dead body, but it proved not to be necessary!

At last Leonard came home on leave, and was looking forward to visiting Beryl.

Leonard to Beryl.

The Rock Hotel,
Llandysul.
May 30 1933.

Dear Beryl,

I got up very early (10.00) this morning for a change, so between now and lunch I'll have plenty of time to concentrate on writing that long letter I promised you.

First, let me thank you for your very nice letter received in Marseilles. I really did answer it from there, but I gave it to the chief operator to post, and he like a silly ass forgot all about it until he was changing into his civvy clothes in London last Friday night. It was too late then to do anything about it, so I thought I'd leave it until I came home.

Taking the voyage as a whole I quite enjoyed our trip from Singapore to London. Most of it I described to you in my letter from Genoa twelve months ago, but in addition to the places mentioned there we called in Aden, Malta and Marseilles as well, so a few remarks concerning these ports may be of interest.

Aden, as you probably know, is an island right at the extreme south west point of Arabia, and at the entrance to the Red Sea. We were due to arrive there in the very late afternoon, and I don't suppose I'll ever forget the beautiful scene that the first glimpse of the place produced.

The bay of Aden itself reached placid and still under the headlands, a dark expanse of turquoise shot with dancing points of light. A faint mist drifted in from the sea, like a shower of fine rain, drenching the glory of the setting sun. In this light, land and sea stood out with cameo-like sharpness beneath the low ceiling of the sky.

I had fallen in love with Aden at first sight, and looked forward to a few pleasant hours crammed with interest when we arrived. My hopes however were doomed to disappointment, and our arrival produced nothing more exciting than a harbour dotted with oil barges; and the town itself seemed merely a few houses scattered haphazardly on the hot, barren slopes of an extinct volcano.

Malta on the other hand was much better. As well as the tour we made of the British Mediterranean Naval Base, the town itself was full of interest. We visited old churches and buildings that dated back to the days of the crusaders, bought a lot of native curios, and listened for hours to the quaint methods of bargaining in the market place. The natives there, too, seemed to enjoy being photographed, and as photography is my second hobby I was quite pleased with our visit.

Of Marseilles I can tell you very little. I was only able to have about an hour ashore in the morning, and it took me all that time to get a stick of shaving soap and a bottle of scent at one of the large stores. You see, they speak French very badly there, which did not seem to fit in with the posh French I learned at school, so when I said "Donnez-moi a stick of shaving soap," the poor blighters merely looked at me in disgust, so I had to resort to the more refined method of grabbing things and shouting "Combien d' argent?" That seemed to work all right, but it took me a long time to get that brainwave!

Anyway, I'm sitting on the lawn at the back of the house writing this letter, and really I've never appreciated the beauty of a Welsh summer so much in my life before. One may travel and see the world, make whoopee in New York or run away from bandits in China, but to really feel at peace with the world, and see nature at its best, one has to come to Wales, and by Wales I mean Llandysul and its environments. I shall be going to Llandrindod for a month on Saturday, but were it not for the fact that I'll be seeing Gertie and Dad, I shouldn't be looking forward to it a bit. My heart's in Llandysul, my thoughts in a little churchyard a few miles outside. One doesn't realise how much one's home means to him until he's been away.

However I'm only boring you now. I should certainly like to visit you sometime but let me know when you are free of engagement. If there are any really interesting photographs to be obtained in that district you might try and remember them; I might be able to make my visit a profitable one photographically as well, then!

Hoping you find life at present as enjoyable as I do, and the very best wishes and kindest regards,

Yours very sincerely,

Len.

Courting Days

One day in June 1933, Leonard cycled down to Newcastle-Emlyn to visit Beryl. Wishing to create a good impression, he had cleaned his bike and polished the seat with brown boot polish. Unfortunately, and unknown to him, the polish transferred to the seat of his white flannels! Beryl tactfully suggested a walk along a quiet country lane where they were unlikely to meet others. This and subsequent meetings relaxed the formality between them. They were falling in love, and their letters became more familiar and intimate.

Even as their lives were finding this new happiness, all was not well in Europe. On August 12 1933, Winston Churchill made his first public speech about the dangers of German rearmament, and his recognition that Nazi Germany represented a terrifying strategic and moral danger. It was in that dark combination, he believed, that the rights, traditions, and fundamental beliefs of Western civilization were already under assault. Parliament seemed unconcerned.

<u>Leonard to Beryl.</u> *Southampton.*
September 6 1934.

Little Sweetheart,

Maggie's stuck in one corner writing to Gertie and Dad, so I'm writing a few lines in case I don't get back early enough to catch the post.

Maggie's enjoying herself immensely. Had lunch on board and we're going to see Grandad at Winchester this afternoon.

Love you lots, darling, and writing long letter tonight.

Your sweetheart,
Leonard XXX

On September 26 1934 the RMS *Queen Mary* was launched at Clydebank. Work on her had been suspended for over two years because of the Depression.

Leonard was now on the m/v *Imperial Transport* (a tanker). The New York Shipping Records show that the ship arrived there on April 7 1935 having sailed from Curacao, Dutch West Indies, on March 30.

On May 6, 1935 the nation celebrated the Silver Jubilee of King George V after twenty-five of the most arduous and troublesome years that had faced any monarch. London was festooned with banners and decorations, parades and pageants were held, and the entire country took part in the rejoicing. Newcastle-Emlyn was no exception.

<u>Beryl to Leonard.</u>

Electra House,
Newcastle-Emlyn.
May 7 1935.

My Darling Sweetheart,

I was so pleased to get your letter from New York yesterday and to know that you'll be home in August. Oh, but it sounds such a long time until you're here! Each time you go back to sea I miss you more, cariad annwyl, and long so much to be with you all the time.

Well, yesterday was Jubilee Day and what a festival it turned out to be! Newcastle-Emlyn was a riot of flags and bunting, flowers and ribbons. It was a glorious sunny day, and most people were given a day off work to celebrate. In the morning, there was a service for all denominations at Bethel chapel, and in the afternoon we had a carnival and pageant with a procession of floats through town led by the

Town Band. I was dressed as a housewife on a float representing the people of the British Empire.

Beryl, left, above the Newcastle-Emlyn Castle archway,
May 6 1935.

We started at the Fair field, went up to Aberarad, and ended up at the castle, with a tableau on the ruins. I managed to scramble up, holding on to the ivy, and pose over the archway with Mary Evans (Sea Ranger) and Phyllis Thomas, (Britannia, complete with helmet, shield and trident!)

The good ladies of the town put on a tea party for the children, who were presented with Jubilee Mugs by Colonel Fitzwilliams. Dad had put in floodlights and in the evening the Castle looked pretty, all lit up. We had a concert with community singing, which ended with "God Save the King" and "Hen Wlad fy Nhadau", then a big bonfire and fireworks to end a very entertaining day. I think we did the King proud! Today's been a bit of an anti-climax with lots of clearing up to do.

Tom is working very hard for his CWB exams. He says he's going to make sure he passes this time – I think that the time he spent working for Dad made him realise he wanted to try a bit harder. I'm also working hard for my Diploma exam in July, so you may soon have a qualified Shorthand teacher for a sweetheart!

The countryside looks very pretty now. With the weather getting warmer, and the long summer evenings coming, I'm just longing to have you all to myself, and to go for long walks, or spend days together at the seaside. Let's hope the weather's still nice in August.

Missing and thinking of you constantly, my love, and may God always bless you and keep you safe, cariad.

Your ever-loving Beryl XXXX

Beryl secured a Teacher's Diploma in Pitman's Shorthand in the July 1935 exam in Bath, and in October commenced as Shorthand Teacher at the Pitman College in London. She stayed at the YWCA at 51 Uxbridge Road, Ealing.

<u>Leonard to Beryl.</u>   *m/v Imperial Transport.*
August 3 1935.

Little Sweetheart,

When I promised to write you the best letter ever yesterday morning, I set myself a very difficult proposition.

Torpedoed Dreams

*Writing to you is not the difficulty: I could do that all night –
pages and pages – but I'm in such a happy mood at the
thought of seeing you soon that I want to convey that mood to
you. However, try as I might I can't find words that
adequately express it, and I do so want to, sweetheart.*

*You see, I'm thinking of all the things that have happened
since I came home from the China coast. Mostly of that
evening when we first visited our little lake, and the
wonderful thing that happened there. I felt awfully shy,
dearest, somehow or other you seemed much too nice a girl
to love me, and I had a vague idea that girls like you only
loved men in story books, yet I was determined to try very
hard, and I'm sure you could have felt my heart beating a
mile away when, not only did you allow my arm to steal
around you, but you also made a slight movement closer to
me, and rested your head so nicely on my shoulder. I could
have shouted with joy darling, and was so happy that it
wasn't until after I'd kissed you that I realised I was on the
wrong side to be really comfortable!*

*I've been trying to live all these little incidents over again
when I'm away from you, dear. Just before I go to sleep at
night I imagine you are nestling close in my arms, but no
matter how hard I concentrate on your actually being there,
my imagination can never reach the standard of reality. Only
you yourself, darling, can thrill me the way any man expects
to be when he's in love, and I'm afraid that imagination is a
very poor substitute indeed for reality.*

*However, dearest, I'm looking forward to next week. We'll
be arriving in Rouen tomorrow evening and out again by
Tuesday evening. It depends then on whether we clean tanks*

or not; if we don't, we'll be in Falmouth on Wednesday and I'll be home probably on Friday, however I'll let you know that from Falmouth and don't forget dearest I'm looking forward terribly to that nice big kiss you've promised me.

And my love is still growing, sweetheart. I thought once that it couldn't, but I suppose it will always grow as long as I have you to love me. You see, darling, it seems to thrive on your love. The more you love me, and show it, the more I love you, and want to show it, and although I've had no opportunity of doing so during the last nine months, I will have very soon now, and you'll be surprised at what a thoroughly capable man I am in that respect.

Sweetheart, it's awfully hard to explain on paper but you'll understand, I know, when I see you again. I like the understanding we have when we're together; there's no need for words then, one just thinks things and automatically somehow the other grasps the idea, and before you know what's happened, thoughts have become reality.

It's simply wonderful to be in love with you, sweetheart, but it will be more wonderful still when we're in a position to call ourselves husband and wife. The thought of you marrying me makes me so happy, dear; well, you see I'd chosen you when we were at school and it only shows what a shrewd judge I must have been even in those days! Since then I've been made to realise more and more how much I have to be thankful for. I've seen the world and seen how the world lives, and somehow I really believe that God must have planned our lives and thrown us together like this, darling.

When Mam died I was very cut up. My sisters were very kind to me, and are all that one can expect sisters to be -

more, really, but I loved dear Mam in a different way and nothing seemed to comfort me until I met you again.

You've filled a big gap in my life, darling. You can never imagine how big a gap it was, but you needn't, dearest, only keep on loving me the way you do and you'll make me very happy then.

I've been very sentimental tonight, but I don't think you'll reprove me. You see I'm so very much in love with you that it's only by being sentimental that I can explain it here. For tonight though I'll stop writing and if there's any news tomorrow I'll write a few more lines again.

Good night darling, and God bless you,
 Your very loving sweetheart,
  Leonard XXXX

The sea-going life, which Leonard had previously really enjoyed, placed a severe limit on the time he and Beryl could spend together, and this, combined with the frustrating scarcity of shore jobs, understandably made him feel rather despondent at times.

Beryl to Leonard.   *51 Uxbridge Road,*
                 Ealing, W5.
             December 15 1935.

Sweetheart Darling,

Thank you for your two lovely last letters (which by the way, were opened by the German Government!) They arrived at mid-day and I was so excited at having them that I could scarcely eat my lunch!

I was pleased to learn you were your own cheerful self

again dearest, as I know what a terrible thing depression is once it gets you in its grip.

Beryl at the YWCA in 1935.

I went down to see my married cousin Violet at Harrow yesterday. She has three lovely children aged 2, 5 and 7 respectively. I wish you could have seen the baby. He is just the sort I would like to have – fat and dimply all over, with blue eyes and fair hair. He crawled all over me and smarmed my face with sticky kisses.

I had lunch and tea there and met my cousin's father in law, aged 80. He is one of the nicest old gentlemen I have ever met. We discussed Robbie Burns most of the afternoon, and then he told me all about his wife (who died two years ago). Apparently he had an ideally happy married life. He told me how they used to sit round the fire and read poetry together (they were both Scottish). Of course I had to tell them all about you, and how much in love we were. My cousin seemed to think that one could never be happy if one was married to a man on sea (but of course I did not agree, and neither did the old gentleman, who said that true love is one of the purest things on God's earth, and that the highest form of love is entirely without sensuality, and that if people are really in love, distance makes no difference.) It was nice to hear him talk and, of course, I should certainly be more prepared to rely on his mature experience than on that of my cousin (who, by the way, is <u>not</u> happily married!)

The wireless is playing some lovely music, dear – dreamy waltzes and tangos. I wish you were here. Let's hope you don't have to make those extra voyages, sweetheart, before getting your leave. I feel I will burst with waiting, sometimes.

My students at the College are getting the Christmas spirit. They pull my leg unmercifully with all sorts of pranks. I go home on Friday. We are going to have a Christmas Party among the College Staff on Thursday evening, and we break up at 12 o'clock the next day.

I'll be thinking of you all over Christmas, cariad, and hope you have a good time. Perhaps we shall be together next year. God bless you dear, and keep you safe always.

Lots and lots of love,
*   Your very loving Beryl XXXXXX*

King George V died on January 20 1936. His son, hitherto the Prince of Wales, was proclaimed King Edward VIII the next day and reigned until December 11 that year amidst much controversy. He wanted to marry Wallis Simpson who was then still married. During the year Wallis divorced her husband Ernest but Parliament would not accept a (twice) divorced woman as queen; the King, being head of the Church of England, had to obey the Church's ban on the marriage of divorced persons while their former spouses were still alive. King Edward was determined to marry Wallis and on December 11 he abdicated the throne. His brother Albert became King George VI.

On May 27 1936 the RMS Queen Mary left Southampton on her maiden voyage to New York.

Engagement

Leonard was on leave and found accommodation in Ealing to be near Beryl. The young lovers were able to enjoy long summer evenings together, dining, dancing, going to the cinema or theatre, or just strolling hand in hand between the magnificent chestnut trees on Ealing Common.

On June 20 1936, a Saturday, they spent the afternoon among the exotic plants in Kew Gardens, admired the beautiful flowers in full bloom, and enjoyed strawberries and cream at a little café. Later, walking Beryl home, Leonard took her in his arms and after kissing her tenderly, proposed to her - and of course, she accepted!

<u>Leonard to Jack and Annie.</u>

5A Grange Road,
Ealing,
London W5.
June 23 1936.

My Dear Mr and Mrs Parkington,

Thank you so much for your consent to my engagement and for the kind wishes conveyed in your letters to Beryl and myself yesterday. It has taken me a long time to write to you, but I know you will forgive the delay. You see, becoming engaged was a new experience to me and I'm not quite certain what one does on such an occasion.

The telephone call on Saturday, I know, was rather sudden, especially as I had only visited you on Thursday evening. However, Friday night was the first time I had really discussed the matter with Beryl, and I wanted to make my position quite clear to her, and make certain she was agreeable first, before seeking your consent.

Both Beryl and I think that an engagement of three, or at the most four years, would be the most suitable. By that time, and assuming I get no further than an operator, I shall probably have attained the position of a senior operator on passenger ships, with fairly short voyages and regular leave, and also the top scale of pay which is £22-15-0 per month. My wages vary somewhat though, according to the class of ship I'm on. So to be practical and not depend on what might happen, I think it best to consider my position as it is at present.

I have about £120-0-0 ready cash that I could lay hands on when it was wanted. This I have saved in spite of a generous allowance to my people at home. My wages on my last ship were £4-16-0 per week, but the very minimum I can earn is £3-9-0 per week. Modern ships however are of a class that it's very seldom one has to drop to that amount, and it's safe to say that my average weekly earnings come to £4-0-0 per week. I have an endowment policy which becomes due in six years time for the sum of £200 plus accumulated profits.

I have promised to assist Raymond to get through Lampeter College, but until we get the result of his London Matriculation Exam, or find out definitely whether he can get a scholarship or not, I don't know how much I shall contribute. Assuming that he gets no scholarship at all I have promised to contribute £7-0-0 per month, but this is strictly a loan, and as soon as he starts earning for himself, will be paid back to me.

However, I know how to shoulder responsibility and save money. I've always lived a clean, sober and honest life, and when it is time for Beryl and me to get married I shall have

£300 to £400 in the bank and £4-0-0 per week on which to start.

I know Beryl deserves much more than this. She's a wonderful girl, and one any man would be proud to marry. The fact that she has chosen to marry me only makes me more determined than ever to work hard for her happiness.

I have tried to make my position quite clear in this letter. Beyond helping Raymond, I have no obligations of any description, but should you think I have forgotten to mention anything, then you can always write for information on that point, or perhaps we can discuss the matter more fully the next time I come home.

Again thanking you for your kindness, and my very best wishes to all,
    Yours very sincerely,
    Leonard.

Jack Parkington to Leonard.

Electra House,
Newcastle-Emlyn.
June 29 1936.

Dear Leonard,

I am delighted to hear in Beryl's letter that you have been lucky enough not to have been called back to the ship yet, and trust that you will get this letter before you sail again.

Referring to your letter of June 23, both my wife and I are pleased at your frank and open statements of your affairs. Continue on these lines with Beryl, and I feel sure the future will bring much-deserved happiness to you both. No doubt from the "little glimpse of Heaven" which you have had during the past week, you will be able to concur with what I say.

Much could be said to the detail in your letter, but most of this can wait until I again have the opportunity of speaking to you personally, and as my prospective son-in-law next time. How about having me for a father-in-law? I suppose you'll risk it?!

Anyway, I'm glad to hear that you have had many nice evenings at Kew, as this is sensible and suits Beryl much better than too much rush and excitement. Look after the "bits" and now you have an objective and a future where you will have all the luck that a wholesome life brings. "Luck" in my view is very largely something which a man can bring about by his own efforts, so "all the best" to you both.

  Yours sincerely,
  "Dad."

P.S. I am enclosing a letter for Beryl from her mother and it includes all I have to say as well. JRP.

All was not roses, however. After the excitement of spending time with Leonard and getting engaged, the prospect of not seeing him for several months left Beryl very depressed, especially as she was living away from home, and she suffered a nervous breakdown. Jack and Annie were understandably concerned about her.

<u>Jack Parkington to Beryl.</u>   *Electra House,*
Newcastle-Emlyn.
October 25 1936.

My dear Beryl,

Torpedoed Dreams

It would be idle for your dear Mother and myself to say that we have not been anxious with regard to you during the past week, but we have surmised that the over-work you had while Leonard was with you has compelled you to take the utmost rest, and trust that you are now beginning to feel more inclined to drop us a few lines (to reassure us) when you can. If it's only a postcard we shall sympathise and understand. Maybe you have written today.

In any case, always remember that this is your home no matter what your circumstances, and it is our earnest desire that you should always have this comforting thought, which we hope you have never lost since the days when you were our funny little kid who liked to poke soap bubbles in the bath.

Now dear, if you feel you are down and a failure remember that this old globe was made to turn. Even dear old (late) Mrs Fitzwilliams who used to be here surrounded with all the luxury and comfort possible was not free from terrible pains at times, and I well remember her saying that she thought these things were sent to try us.

Old friend Bonny Hughes always said "No Cross, No Crown". So we must hope and struggle on, always remembering that we live for others also.

Trusting to hear from you when you feel better, and hoping matters are not too bad.

   With our fondest love,
    Yours always,
     Dad XXXX

When Beryl recovered she started a new job and became

secretary to Bernard Sunley, a millionaire who had risen from very modest origins to be the founder and managing director of Sunley's, a large earthmoving and construction company. Though he was an astute businessman, his literacy left something to be desired, and Beryl attended to the correspondence and assisted with the running of the business. She worked for Sunley's until she left to get married.

Leonard's elder sister Maggie married Edmond Swete at the end of 1936. He taught French at Llandysul County School, had taught Leonard and Beryl there, and lodged at the Rock Hotel. Born in India of Irish parents, he had been wounded at Gallipoli in the First World War and was considerably older than Maggie.

With their wedding in view, Jack and Annie wondered where Leonard and Beryl would be able to make their home, and kindly offered to accommodate them at *Electra House*. However, much as they appreciated the offer, the young couple wanted to live independently, and agonised over how to tell Beryl's parents tactfully. In the end, Beryl broke it to them, and Leonard followed up with a letter.

<u>Leonard to Jack and Annie.</u>   *s/s Holmbury,*
Basra,
Iraq.
December 23 1936.

My Dear Mr and Mrs Parkington,
I am writing to thank you for the very kind and generous proposal you have made, that Beryl and I should make our home with you after we are married.
Please excuse my delay in writing. I really intended doing

so immediately we arrived here, but unfortunately I contracted rather a bad attack of fever which kept me in bed for ten days, and later I thought it better to wait a little longer until after Beryl had been home and talked things over with you. She could then explain much better than ever I could in a letter our attitude towards the proposal.

By now, of course, she will have done this, and it only remains for me to thank you for the kind spirit in which the proposal was made, and also for the helpful advice you have given us. You can be sure that when our plans for the wedding are a little more definite we will bear this in mind, and allow ourselves to be guided by your experience.

We have been in this part of the world nearly a month now, and I cannot imagine any place that is less interesting. Even the scenery lacks beauty and as far as I can see the whole country is just a desert with a little fertile soil on the river bank, where dates and wheat are cultivated.

Christmas will be upon us in just another two days, and I'm wondering what it will be like out here. I'd much rather have spent it at home, though. Do you know, it's seven years since I did that last, and this will be the first time since I've been at sea that I shall spend it in port. One consolation however is that the weather here is quite cool at present. Every ship makes a special effort to prepare a really thrilling Christmas dinner, and when the temperature is around 80 or 90 in the shade, the effort is wasted as one cannot appreciate turkey and plum pudding under these conditions!

I'm looking forward to a really happy Christmas next year, though. If all goes well I hope to be financially sound enough by then for Beryl and me to be married. I'm saving hard with that end in view, and with a little luck can manage it quite nicely. So far however, Beryl and I have agreed to keep this arrangement to ourselves, so that if anything should happen to interfere with our plans there'll be no gossip. Later on we can be more definite, but for the present I think this plan is the best, don't you?

Again thanking you for the kindness you have always shown me, and wishing you health and happiness in the New Year,

> *Yours very sincerely,*
> *Leonard.*

<u>Jack Parkington to Beryl and Leonard.</u> *Electra House, Newcastle-Emlyn. Feb 23 1937.*

My dear Beryl and Leonard,

I am pleased to hear that you are together again, and to have received your dual letter recently. Thank you very much for the little cigars which came to hand when all else seemed taboo.

I lost rather a lot of blood last week, and on Sunday the great Dr Budd performed a minor operation, the result of which I hope will put a stop to further blood-letting for a time. He says the latter was probably good for me, as my blood pressure is now normal, but added that of course there was a limit to blood loss.

I can just understand poor Leonard getting "stuck" in his letter. Do you think it possible for any poor chap to carry on with Beryl around? Father could never do it!

You do not state in your letter how long Leonard will be

staying, but I trust that you will both have a good time and not get over-fatigued. There is plenty to improve the shining hour without racing all over the shop.

Now I am getting at a loss as what to say next because Beryl isn't here! The shop door bell rings, a person appears and I can't even swear!

Bye bye, it's nearly 6.30 pm.
Yours always,
Dad.

On March 8 1937, Prince Edward, the abdicated Edward VIII, was created Duke of Windsor. His brother Albert was crowned King George VI at Westminster Abbey on May 12, and on June 3, the Duke of Windsor and Wallis Simpson were married in exile at the Château de Candé in France, she then becoming the Duchess of Windsor.

Marriage

After some uncertainties about Leonard's shipping arrangements, he and Beryl fixed their Wedding for Monday, December 20 1937. Beryl had made all the arrangements for the day, and gave Leonard strict instructions that he was not to see her before she arrived at the church, as it was considered to be unlucky.

Leonard, Fred, Gertie and Raymond travelled down from Llandysul in a hired car, dropping Gertie off at Electra House to join Beryl and her three other bridesmaids before continuing to Holy Trinity Church at the end of its lane. It was a blustery day, but the rain kept away.

The Daimler limousine from Cawdor Garage was on hand to transport the bride-to-be and her attendants once they were dressed to everyone's satisfaction. Annie, Jack and Tom had already walked the short distance to the church; Beryl took Jack's arm at the gate. As they made their way indoors and up the aisle Miss Pattie Maurice, the organist, struck up the Wedding March from *Lohengrin*. Beryl looked radiantly happy as she took her place beside Leonard, who was beaming with joy. Beryl was given away by Jack, and the Rev Howell Rosser officiated.

After the service, the church bells rang out joyfully as the newly-weds made their way through a snowstorm of confetti thrown by the throng of well-wishers lining the pathway through the churchyard. The cars drove slowly back up the lane, to be stopped every few yards by urchins holding ropes across until pennies were thrown to them – a time-honoured local tradition!

It was only a short drive to the reception at the Emlyn

Arms Hotel. Harold Squibbs, the photographer from Cardigan, took photographs and the bridal party and guests enjoyed a substantial luncheon. Several speeches were made and telegrams read out.

The wedding cake was decorated with a ship; somehow this fell off during the festivities, and years later Beryl sadly recalled someone saying it was a bad omen.

With the reception over, after final kisses and hugs from their guests, the limousine took the happy couple to the railway station at the top end of town, where a reserved compartment awaited them on the afternoon train to Carmarthen. As it puffed slowly away, its whistle echoed and re-echoed from the surrounding hills, and detonators exploded under its wheels to cheer them on their way.

They spent their wedding night at Cardiff before a very short honeymoon in London. Leonard had to be in Southampton less than a week later to join his ship.

A NEWCASTLE-EMLYN BRIDE. A pretty wedding was solemnised at Holy Trinity Church, Newcastle-Emlyn on Monday December 20 between Miss Beryl Parkington, only daughter of Mr and Mrs JR Parkington, Electra House, Newcastle-Emlyn and Mr Leonard Frederick Ball, elder son of Mr FH Ball and the late Mrs Ball, 2 Fairhaven, Temple Avenue, Llandrindod Wells. The Vicar, Rev Howell Rosser, officiated, and Miss Pattie Maurice was at the organ.

Given away by her father, the bride wore a dress of ivory satin with a slight train, and a veil held in place by orange blossom. She carried a shower bouquet of lilies

Rear, L-R: Jack, Fred, Raymond, Tom, Rev Howell Rosser.
Front: Annie, Bethan Jenkins, Rayda Jones, Leonard, Beryl, Molly Pritchard, Gertie.

of the valley and violets, and wore pearls (a gift from the bridegroom). There were four bridesmaids: Miss Rayda Jones (chief bridesmaid), Miss Molly Pritchard (cousin), Miss Gertie Ball (sister of bridegroom), and Miss Bethan Jenkins (cousin). The latter wore a dress of rose satin and a garland of violets, and carried a posy of the same flowers. The other three wore rose velvet dresses, with belts and caps of violets. Each carried a muff of rose velvet trimmed with violets. The bridesmaids each wore a silver bracelet (a gift from the bridegroom). Mr Raymond Ball (brother of the bridegroom) was best man, and Mr Tom Parkington and Mr Lionel Rose the groomsmen.

After the ceremony a reception was held at the Emlyn Arms Hotel, at which speeches were made by Mr D Roy Evans; Rev John Philips; Rev JC Davies; Rev H Rosser; Mrs James, Barclays Bank; Mrs IT Hughes, Llandysul, and others. Numerous congratulatory telegrams were read out by the best man. After the reception, the happy couple left for their honeymoon. Over one hundred wedding presents were received, the families of both bride and bridegroom being well-known and respected.

(From the *Western Telegraph and Cymric Times,* Dec 23 1937.)

Leonard continued to be appointed to different ships by Marconi, and was generally only able to spend brief periods at home before being assigned to other voyages. He and Beryl did however manage to have a short holiday together. In June 1938 she joined him on a ship at Cardiff and travelled with him to Glasgow. They spent a week at Ardrossan, a quiet harbour town on the Firth of Clyde.

Fred and Gertie were still living and working in Llandrindod Wells. Gertie had bought a little car, an Austin Seven which she called *Thunderbox*, and they had been for a trial run.

<u>Fred and Gertie to Leonard.</u>

2 Fairhaven,
Llandrindod Wells.
July 24 1938.

Dear Leonard,

Thought I'd drop you a few lines today. We were very glad to get your letter from Cardiff and to hear that you have a good ship. We also had a letter from Beryl, and she seems to be patting herself on the back because the cook comes from the Newcastle-Emlyn district, so she is sure you'll get plenty to eat!

Well, we had a lovely journey back from Llandysul that Sunday. It started to rain just after we left Pencader and it simply poured all the way. Just as we reached the top of Sugar Loaf we ran out of petrol, but as you know, we had a spare tin in the car and the rain stopped for just a few minutes so we were able to put that in the tank without getting any water in it, but then the rain came on harder than ever.

We had hardly any traffic and at one point I noticed the speedometer needle just touching 50 mph – your little sister is getting to be a speed merchant! Our average speed for the whole journey worked out at 26.8 miles per hour; that's good going. Petrol worked out at 35 miles per gallon so the little bus isn't too expensive to run. I don't believe that Gertie would be any more pleased if somebody gave her a Rolls Royce. She went to Aberystwyth and Borth last Sunday but today she isn't going anywhere. I'll hand over to Gertie now, or she'll say I've left nothing for her to tell you, so

Cheerio and All the Best from
Dad XX

My dear Leonard,

Since Dad has told you so much about the little bus I must tell you more! Actually, on that journey she did 35 to the gallon on petrol, but now Dad's done something to the timing, so we hope to get about 40 or more to the gallon.

After the motorcycle reliability trials came through here last week there was a lot of spare petrol. You see, the petrol firms supplied petrol free of charge to the competitors, and after they went there was a lot left over, so some bright individual started selling it cheaply. I got eleven gallons for 10/6 – less than 1/- a gallon and I normally pay 1/7. As everyone says, this is the very best stuff – they wouldn't have inferior petrol at reliability trials!

Yesterday I received a notice that I am to take my driving test at 4pm on 10th August, but I've just written to ask them if they can take me during my lunch hour or after 6pm as I can't get time off at 4 o'clock. After all the tales I've heard I haven't much hope of passing the first time, but of course, one never knows!

Must close now, to catch tonight's post.
With all my love,
Gertie XXX

Gertie not only passed her driving test with flying colours, but later her calm and encouraging disposition helped her become a very capable driving instructor.

On September 29 1938, Prime Minister Neville Chamberlain, with all the naiveté of a village parson negotiating with the Mafia, signed the shameful Munich Agreement and a resolution with Germany determining to resolve all future disputes between the two countries through peaceful means. He returned to London the next day waving the paper bearing the resolution and made his *Peace For Our Time* speech.

Wireless Greetings Telegram from Leonard to Beryl.
(First Wedding Anniversary.)

s/s Felldene.   *20/12/38*
Mrs Ball Electra House Newcastle-Emlyn Carms

HAPPY THOUGHTS AND LOVING GREETINGS DARLING MANY THANKS FOR BIRTHDAY MESSAGE LEONARD

Leonard to Beryl.   *s/s Lyminge,*
Genoa.
June 4 1939.

My own darling wife,
Many thanks for the nice letters I received here this morning, cariad. I was very sorry to hear of the sunburn trouble and trust it has healed nicely by now. Don't try to get brown too quickly beloved, a little sun every day does more good than a lot at once, and also you won't peel if you tan

gradually.

We've had some glorious weather this voyage darling, but unfortunately I've been much too busy to enjoy it properly. Most of the time I've been finishing off my accommodation so that my time will be more free after we leave this port.

In Llandrindod Wells, 1939.

For all my industry though, it did not stop me from thinking of you and missing you very much indeed, darling. I brought away such wonderful memories and I enjoyed my last leave such a lot that I'm missing it all more than I can tell you on paper, sweetheart.

You've been a darling and entertained me so well; you

choose nice walks and cook nice meals, and you've reciprocated my love to such an extent that I think of it all every day, long for it too, dear, and anxiously look forward to the end of this voyage and our next meeting. (Remainder missing).

<u>Beryl to Leonard.</u>

19 Fraser Road,
Greenford,
Middx.
August 24 1939.

My own very dear Leonard,

I've been puzzling as to how to get in touch with you at Cardiff to give you more detailed instructions as to how to get here. It isn't difficult really, once you know the way.

You see, I've already got a job at £3-5-0 a week (starting Monday 28th) with the GEC at Wembley. They say they are giving me a 3 months' trial before increasing it to £3-10-0. It's not very far from here – a 2d bus ride.

But the snag is, sweetheart, I may not be able to meet you at Paddington as I had very much hoped. On the other hand, I still hope to be there to welcome you, my darling.

I shall be free at 6 pm each evening (5.30 pm some days) and 1 pm on Saturdays.

I can meet you after these times, my darlingest, so I could meet the 3.21 pm, 5.12 pm, 6.05 pm, 6.28 pm, 9.33 pm, 10.38 pm, 10.56 pm which arrive at Paddington at 7.15 pm, 8.20 pm, 9.40 pm, 2.40 am, 3.25 am and 7.20 am respectively.

If you can come before these times, Ieuan (my cousin from Newcastle-Emlyn) will meet you at Paddington if you arrive on or before Saturday September 3 (he is staying until then).

You had better wire me at this address (put in c/o Jenkins, 19 Fraser Road, Greenford, Middx) saying what time you expect to arrive at Paddington, dear.

If you wish to phone, it is Perivale 3665 but that's my aunt's number at 75 Manor Farm Road. I'm not actually staying there, but they'll willingly take a message if they're in.

Cariad annwyl, I do hope there won't be a GWR train strike – that would be a calamity. However, I dare say there will be an emergency service running, or a bus service from Cardiff; or perhaps Gertie would run you up if you paid her expenses. She could stay here and I would of course pay for all her board, lodging, etc. But I don't want you to bother her if you can manage some other way.

I feel confident there can't possibly be a war. There are a horrible lot of jittery people around here, but Winnie is ever so cool. We are out of the danger zone at Wembley.

Keep a brave heart, my darlingest. I want you so very much nowadays. Just to talk things over with you and, more than that, to give you all my love. You know how deep my love is, sweetheart. God willing, the plans we have made are well on their way to fruition. My only fear is that I am tying myself to a job and shan't be able to see you as much as I want – but we'll both have to sacrifice for a short time, at any rate, if we want to be together always.

Our future is in God's hands, my dear dear husband, but remember whatever happens, whatever calamities may come, I love you always.

Looking forward to having a happy time with you soon, my dearest,

Your own wife, Beryl XXXXXX

War

The storm clouds of World War 2 were gathering over Europe. People were desperately hoping that it would not eventuate, but on August 24 the Emergency Powers (Defence) Act 1939 gave full authority to defence regulations. Parliament was recalled, Army reservists called up and Civil Defence workers placed on alert. On August 30 the evacuation of children from major cities began.

Germany invaded Poland on September 1 1939, and Britain declared war on Germany two days later. People's worst fears were realised, and the relentless turmoil began.

Maggie and Edmond took in two motherless Liverpool sisters, Nora and Joanie, as evacuees for the duration of the War. They found life in Llandysul very different from what they'd previously known, but gradually settled in. (After the War, Joanie didn't want to leave, and Maggie and Edmond adopted her.)

On November 29, Beryl's brother Tom married Kitty Davies of Pencader. They too had been classmates at Llandysul County School. Tom was now in the Royal Navy and based in Portsmouth.

In December 1939, Annie's sister Emily, a childless widow, died. She left her house to Graig, the Baptist chapel which her family attended. Annie had some savings and bought the house from the chapel for her and Jack's retirement, but also so that in the meantime, Beryl and Leonard might have a home of their own.

Situated at 4 Castle Street, only about 150 yards from *Electra House*, it was the end house of a terrace of four. There was a sitting room, a living room and a kitchen, with two bedrooms upstairs. As was common at the time, there was an outside toilet but no bathroom (the one at *Electra House* was at their disposal.) The front door opened on to the street; at the back a long narrow garden sloped down to an oxbow in the River Teifi with a picturesque view to the hills beyond.

The young people were overjoyed at Annie's kindness, and Beryl set about cleaning and decorating to welcome Leonard home in February 1940. They spent his leave happily, painting, looking at furniture, planning how they would arrange the rooms, and hoping to start a family.

The war rolled on relentlessly. On January 1 1940, Britain called up two million 19- to 27-year-olds for military service.

Less than a third of the food available in Britain at the start of the war was produced at home. Enemy ships and submarines immediately began to target incoming Allied merchant vessels, preventing vital supplies - including fruit, sugar, cereals and meat - from reaching the UK. In addition to his long absences, Leonard's life was now frequently in danger in the Merchant Navy. A time of continual worry began for Beryl, who because of censorship, never knew where he was bound, or if he was safe. Henceforth, his letters could tell her nothing of his experiences abroad.

King George VI issued this message:

"In these anxious days I would like to express to all Officers and Men in the British Merchant Navy and the British Fishing Fleets my confidence in their unfailing determination to play their vital part in defence. To each one I would say: Yours is a task no less essential to my people's experience than that allotted to the Navy, Army and Air

Force. Upon you the Nation depends for much of its foodstuffs and raw materials and for the transport of its troops overseas. You have a long and glorious history, and I am proud to bear the title "Master of the Merchant Navy and Fishing Fleets". I know that you will carry out your duties with resolution and with fortitude, and that high chivalrous traditions of your calling are safe in your hands. God keep you and prosper you in your great task."

Official rationing began on January 8 1940 with bacon, butter and sugar. To ensure fair distribution of supplies, the Ministry of Food issued ration books containing coupons to every person, and families had to register at one shop. Rations were distributed by weight, monetary value or points. The shopkeeper was provided with enough food for registered customers. Purchasers had to take ration books with them when shopping, so the relevant coupon or coupons could be cancelled. One person's typical *weekly* allowance would be: one fresh egg; 4oz margarine and bacon (about four rashers); 2oz butter and tea; 1oz cheese; and 8oz sugar. Meat was allocated by price, so cheaper cuts became popular. Points could be pooled or saved to buy pulses, cereals, tinned goods, dried fruit, biscuits and jam. Prices were fixed by the government, so profiteering could not take place.

People were encouraged to "Dig for Victory" and every garden and allotment sprouted fruit and vegetables which the owners could consume or barter. Rabbits and chickens were raised on kitchen scraps, and wild rabbits shot or trapped. Fred was an expert gardener, and had a large allotment on the New Road at Llandysul. Thanks to his industry, the family was never short of a good supply of fruit and vegetables. Ironically, the overall health of the nation actually improved under rationing, as practically everyone received an adequate if not sumptuous diet.

<u>Leonard to Beryl.</u> *(Ship's name suppressed).*
February 19 1940.

My darling Wife,

Just a few lines to let you know we've arrived safely and to tell you, too, how much I have been thinking of you and longing for you, dearest.

It is barely a week since we were last together, cariad, and yet I don't think I ever remember time passing so very, very slowly. I'm so very anxious to get back to help you with our new home dearest, and such a lot of ideas have been passing through my mind that I'm bursting to talk them over with you.

The weather during the last two days has been quite warm and spring-like, reminding me of happy days we have spent together at this time of the year, cariad. When I am next home spring will really be with us, and in addition to the added interest of our new home, I'm looking forward to taking you for nice walks where we can gather flowers and admire nature's awakening after her long winter sleep.

For the present, the approximate date of our arrival is as I told you before leaving, darling. We're keeping well to schedule and if I'm not actually handling a paint brush on St David's Day, I shall be doing so the following day, I'm sure.

How are your ideas progressing, darling? Has the dining room suite arrived in good condition, and the carpet; and does the latter look as nice at home as it did in the shop?

I want to ask a thousand questions like this, but I'll have to be patient and wait until I get home before I shall find the answers.

My studies are progressing nicely, and I've done two lessons and have a third started. I hope I can sit my exams this year all right, and am very confident of passing.

Roll on time and let me get home soon. I'm feeling as homesick as can be, more this voyage than I've ever been, sweetheart. I have such a lot to look forward to, and such a dear little wife waiting to welcome me home.
(Remainder missing).

On May 10, Neville Chamberlain resigned as Prime Minister, and was replaced by Winston Churchill. Once he had taken office, Churchill wrote that he felt he was "walking with destiny". Three days later he told the House of Commons that he had "nothing to offer but blood, toil, tears and sweat", and set the mood of the nation by declaring that the British aim was "Victory. Victory at all costs. Victory in spite of all terror. Victory, however long and hard the road may be, for without victory there is no survival."

The Battle of Britain began on July 9 1940 and ended on October 31, and Churchill paid tribute in Parliament to the Royal Air Force: "Never in the field of human conflict was so much owed by so many to so few." By preventing Germany from gaining air superiority, the battle ended the threat that Hitler would launch Operation Sea Lion, a proposed amphibious and airborne invasion of Britain.

Family-wise, Leonard's sister Gertie married Cecil Thomas, another native of Newcastle-Emlyn, in Llandysul on

July 9, and Kitty, Tom's wife, gave birth to my cousin Barbara at *Electra House* on November 7.

Britain continued to be pounded by *Luftwaffe* bombs. On November 14, Coventry was blitzed and the centre destroyed – 500 bombers dropped 150,000 incendiaries, 503 tons of high explosives and 130 parachute mines, levelling 60,000 buildings and killing 568 people. The blitz continued through the month and into December: Birmingham, West Bromwich, Dudley, Tipton, Southampton, Bristol, Plymouth, Sheffield, Liverpool and Manchester were heavily bombed, with hundreds of people killed and many more injured.

Then on December 29, heavy bombing caused the Second Great Fire of London, the largest continuous area of Blitz destruction anywhere, with the area destroyed being greater than that of the Great Fire of London in 1666. The raid was timed to coincide with a particularly low tide on the River Thames, making water difficult to obtain for fire fighting. Over 1,500 fires were started, with many joining up to form three major conflagrations which in turn caused a fire storm that spread the flames further. More than 160 civilians died; many more died of their injuries in the days that followed.

Leonard was home on leave again in January 1941. Beryl and he were keen to start a family, and I was evidently conceived during this time!

On February 19, the Swansea Blitz began. Ironically, the Three Nights Blitz in February 1941 and numerous other bombing sorties over the town left the docks and industries (the main targets) virtually unscathed, but the town centre was completely obliterated. 230 people were killed and 409 injured.

Due to the 56,000 incendiary bombs used, the fires burned continuously and a bright glow could be seen in the south eastern sky at night from Newcastle-Emlyn, 60 miles distant. Annie's sister Sue, who lived in Swansea, recalled running down the street in terror with incendiary bombs falling nearby.

The year went by with Leonard facing frequent dangers, having miserably short and infrequent breaks at home, then having to return to his ship. Letters were the only means for him and Beryl to express their longing for each other, and they were unreliable, with no guarantee that they would be delivered at all.

<u>Leonard to Beryl.</u> *(Ship's name suppressed).*
September 26 1941.

My Darling Wife,

Forgive me for ending my letter so abruptly last night, dearest. The Captain came back and, as usual, there was lots of work to be done immediately. I wasn't paid until it was too late to catch the PO open to register the money so I telegraphed it early this morning (it was £12-0-0). If I'd had time I would have collected another month's pay that became due today, from the Marconi office. But we left at noon and I couldn't manage it, dear.

My goodness, time has gone slowly since I left home, cariad. If my leave had only passed as slowly it would have lasted a month. I've missed you more than I can say dearest. Somehow or other I can hardly realise that we really spent four whole days together, and a few odd hours besides. Now it seems as though it were only four hours, and I'm so looking forward to my next leave.

We're quite a happy family here now – only the Chief Engineer is new. The Captain and Mate have of course been here before. I don't think you know Captain Davies, but you've met Thomas, while the Chief Engineer seems to be quite a decent fellow.

Cariad fach, I do wish I were home with you. Yesterday and today I've been having some very bad bouts of homesickness. I'm not worried when I write thus, dearest, but I'm missing you so very much and naturally, darling, I wish that at this time I could relieve you of the burden of my being away from home. Keep your little chin up and a brave heart. Don't let the events of our last voyage worry you, as it's quite possible that we'll be another year at sea without experiencing anything again. We're in God's care, beloved, and I've always had faith that He will protect us. There's no reason whatever why we should break that faith now, is there dear?

If I'm not home before the happy event takes place darling, here's wishing you the very best, and hoping that our little one will be someone sweet and dear like its mother. I honestly have no preference where its sex is concerned, no matter how seriously I consider it – all I want is someone who will have a full share of its mother's character and sweetness.

I don't know when we are leaving finally, dearest. I shall post this letter on my way to the conference tomorrow morning. I may have time to write again before I leave, but don't count too much on that, dear.

You know I love you from the very bottom of my heart. I'm missing you more than I can describe tonight, but when we next meet I shall do my utmost to make up for it all, darling.

Keep your little chin up and don't worry more than you can help, cariad fach. In six weeks from now you can look forward to seeing me again and if I haven't succeeded in expressing my love quite as nicely as I'd like to, I'll try to do it then.

Lots and lots of love and kisses darling.
May God bless you and keep you safe always, my dear.
Your very, very loving husband,
Leonard XXXX

Beryl's pregnancy had less than a month to go.

Beryl to Leonard.   *4 Castle Street,*
Newcastle-Emlyn.
October 4 1941.

Sweetheart Darling,
Just another note to cheer you on arrival, dear. I do hope it arrives in time and that you will have more than my first letter to greet you.

I've been ever so busy all the week getting ready for Baby. Mother and I made 24 nappies, and washed these together with 12 ready-made ones I had bought at Bridge Shop. I've been enamelling the furniture in the back bedroom in baby blue, and putting the finishing touches to nighties, etc. In addition, the house has had to be thoroughly cleaned, so I've had a busy time! Fortunately I am still keeping fit, though I get rather stiff at times, as you may guess.

How I long for you, my very dearest, to be with me now and to share in the joys of preparation. But I must not grumble, so long as you are safe and well. That is what I pray for most in these days of danger. My thoughts go with you wherever you are, beloved. I only wish I could be with you in person as well as in thought.

Nurse tells me I have not got a very big baby so far – let's hope it keeps tiny, till after it's born, as that will make things so much easier for me. I shall go to see Dr Budd for an examination in a week's time. Meantime, dearest, keep your spirits high, and don't worry about me. We are all in God's hands and can only leave things with Him. However, I know you cannot help being a bit anxious over this, our first little one. I am in very good health and that counts for a lot.

Let us hope you'll soon be back again and then you will be able to satisfy yourself as to how things are going, beloved.

Your papers from Bennett's College have come back and you have a pass on the Exam Paper – 88%, jolly good!

Sweetheart, I send all my love with this letter and want to thank you, once again, for all the happiness you have brought me.

God bless you and keep you safe, beloved.
Your own little wife,
Beryl
XXXX

<u>Beryl to Leonard.</u>

4 Castle Street,
Newcastle-Emlyn.
October 14 1941.

Sweetheart Darling,
It was such a relief to get your cable this morning and to know you had arrived safely. My one regret is, dear, that

owing to the enclosed letter being returned by the censor, there won't be one to greet you abroad. However, I actually wrote two, so perhaps he has let the second one go through.

I am looking forward to seeing you again more than I can tell, cariad. It would be such a comfort to have you here now. The last month is always a trying time, even if one is in good health (as I undoubtedly am).

I went to see Dr Budd for an examination on Saturday and apparently the baby is in the correct position now (head downward) although not in the most ideal, as it is back to front. However, this is nothing serious, but it generally means that labour lasts longer. I have to go for another examination in a week's time, and if Dr is not satisfied then, will have to go to Carmarthen to Dr James at the Clinic for a second opinion. By then I shall know whether I am to go into hospital or not. If not, we have already made alternative arrangements for me to be at home. As you know, dearest, Rayda's nurse will do her best to come, also Gertie and Kitty have very kindly promised, and there's always Mother to take any responsibility, so really I'm very fortunate, though I naturally can't help wishing you were here.

So you see, sweetheart, I am looking forward more than ever to seeing you once more. You always make me so happy when you are here.

I've been putting the finishing touches in blue to the back bedroom and am jolly glad to finish as I cannot carry on with anything for any length of time! It is uncomfortable to sit or stand for very long and I rest every afternoon. Apparently, everyone feels like this when at my stage.

By the way, dear, I shall be transferring some money from

the PO to our bank account because it will be more accessible there, and we shall have several cheques to pay out. Thought you'd like to know.

Please forgive this scrappy letter, my very dearest. I love you so much and yet the words don't seem to flow as they should. You have always made me so happy.

Till I next write then, cheerio cariad. I want the time to fly by until you're here again.

God bless and keep you, darling.
Your very own, very loving
Beryl XXXX

<u>Beryl to Leonard.</u>

4 Castle Street,
Newcastle-Emlyn.
October 26 1941.

Leonard Dearest,

It was so nice of you to cable me on my Birthday – I had such a thrill when I saw the message. Thank you so much, darling.

It will be so nice to see you once again, beloved – next to that, waiting for your letters, very impatiently I'm afraid, is one of my main interests.

Of course, there is the coming infant to keep me occupied too, sweetheart – though you know its Daddy will always come first.

I went to Carmarthen hospital last Friday for an examination and X-ray, and the doctor there advises me to come in on November 1st for an induction, as my measurements are a bit small. That means the babe may be persuaded to come into the world a fortnight or so before time. The treatment, I'm told, consists of large doses of castor oil (!!!) plus quinine and hot baths – nothing more drastic as they don't believe in surgical inductions for first babies.

If that doesn't work, they'll send me home again and wait until I go into labour on my own, and then I shall go into hospital for a trial labour. If this doesn't produce results, they will give me a Caesarean section.

There is nothing at all to worry about, sweetheart darling, but I think it wise to take Dr Budd's advice and that of Dr James (the hospital doctor). These measures are purely precautionary, dearest, and I am told they won't do the baby any harm and will also be better for me. You'll know I'll be getting the very best attention, cariad. Maybe nothing further than the induction will be necessary.

I saw Kitty in Carmarthen, where she is staying with her cousin. Rayda and she and I had coffee and cakes together. Barbara can crawl now, and also imitates all sorts of noises. Her birthday is on 7th November. Tom is still at sea.

I'm keeping jolly well, dear. Went for a walk with Mother this afternoon and hoped to reach our lake, but couldn't manage the distance. However, all the romantic associations came into my mind, cariad, and I thought of you and our love for each other – the most wonderful thing in the world. We are always so happy together, aren't we darling, and I look back upon this year as being one of the happiest in my life.

May God bless and keep you safe, beloved.

Your very own wife and sweetheart,

Beryl

XXXX

P.S. Do try to get enough coupons for an overcoat from the BOT darling, failing which please bring your Navy overcoat with you – it is warmer than a mac.

<u>Leonard to Beryl.</u> *(Ship's name suppressed but Gibraltar stamps on envelope).*
October 28 1941.

Cariad Annwyl,

We're due to arrive in port again early in the morning so I thought I'd get a letter ready for posting on arrival.

I have been thinking about you very much indeed since I last wrote, dearest. For one thing we can't possibly arrive now in time for the happy event, and I would have liked to have been near you.

The other reason of course is that I'm missing you so very, very much indeed. I can't find words to express how intense has been my longing to be with you. This is easily the loneliest voyage I have ever made, sweetheart, even though the present company of officers is perhaps the most congenial I have ever sailed with.

I shan't be a bit sorry to see the end of this voyage, cariad, and I'm getting so excited too. I've been hoping and hoping that things would get along and that I'd have every reasonable chance of being home in time for the birth of our first little one. I did so want to see you as soon as I should have been allowed to, darling, and of course dear, I should have wanted to see our little one too.

But I suppose it's no use letting the disappointment hit me too hard, beloved. You'll be disappointed too, or were you really hoping that I'd arrive after it was all over? You did mention the latter, cariad, but I don't think you were very sure of what you wanted at the time.

Anyway, beloved, here's wishing you the very best of luck, and hoping that everything will be quite normal. Don't worry because I'm away, but look forward to the proud moment when you'll be introducing me to our first born. I don't know for certain when that will be cariad, but at present say within about ten days of the date you fixed for its arrival. We're not expecting any more delays darling, but I can't get more definite information than that until we arrive tomorrow.

Cariad fach, rwy'n meddwl cymaint amdanat ti y dyddiau 'ma! My heart is so very full of love, yet my power of expressing it seems so feeble, darling. It's so wonderful to think that something we've wanted for such a very, very long time will soon be ours, and so comforting to know that it will have the best little mother in the world.

I've always been proud of my dear little wife. When I meet her this time home, I shall be fairly bursting with it. I still don't care two hoots whether it's a son or a daughter, darling, so if you've developed any preference since I left home I hope your wish comes true.

We've been having delightful weather lately – fine and warm, but not too warm. I've spent lots of time on deck and am quite sunburnt. My health too has been very good and we've had no unpleasant experiences of any kind.

I'm looking forward now, dear, to our next meeting. I don't know yet where we are going, but wherever it is you can bet I shan't waste any time about getting home.

Meantime cariad fach, keep your little chin up and look forward to my return. I love you from the bottom of my heart dearest, and shall be thinking of you every day. If we were together now I could express my love far better than I can manage on paper, but perhaps if you take your own love for me and realise that I reciprocate it fully, you will realise how very much I do love you.

Goodnight and God bless you, beloved, and may He keep you safe always.

Lots and lots of love from your very, very loving husband,
    Leonard XXXX

<u>Beryl to Leonard.</u>
    4 Castle Street,
    Newcastle-Emlyn.
    October 31 1941.

Sweetheart Darling,

Thanks ever so much for your nice Air Mail letter received yesterday. I was glad to learn you were safe and well, and am now looking forward to seeing you again.

This letter is just to wish you the very happiest Birthday ever, cariad, and all my love accompanies my good wishes. I hope to present you with a son or daughter as a birthday gift, dear, but just in case that doesn't happen in time, am knitting you a present as well.

As mentioned in my previous letter, I'm going into hospital tomorrow, but as you know, the treatment may not work and I may have to come out again until things happen naturally.

Gertie came down yesterday and gave me a box of sweets as a birthday present. They will be very useful to take away the taste of the castor oil and other drugs which I shall have in hospital! All are well at Llandysul. I understand Raymond was not sitting his exams in October as intended, as only those who had tried before were allowed to try then.

It will be lovely to see you once more sweetheart, and to be with you again.

Do try and get those coupons for an overcoat and whatever else you need. I say "coupons" but what you really get is a permit, I believe. I enclose a letter from Mr Davies which explains clearly.

I am feeling ever so well and happy, so don't worry about me will you, dear? I am so fortunate in having enjoyed perfect health during the waiting time, as it could have been such an unhappy period if I had been ill and helpless.

Will do my best to write you from hospital, sweetheart. You know my love for you increases whenever I see you, dearest, and I always look forward to being with you once more. My married life has been the happiest time I can remember, and since we have moved into our own home and are expecting our first little one, things have seemed almost perfect – I say "almost" because with you away, they could not be completely so.

May God bless and keep you safe, dearest. I shall be thinking of you in the rather blank days to come, and the knowledge of your love will, as always, cheer me and give me courage. I love you.

> *Your own*
> *Beryl XXXX*

Parenthood

<u>**Greetings Telegram from Annie to Beryl.**</u>

NEWCASTLE-EMLYN   November 4 1941   11.25

Mrs Ball County Infirmary Maternity Unit CARMARTHEN

WELCOME   LITTLE   STRANGER   SEE   YOU
WEDNESDAY NAIN XX

(There are two Welsh words for "Granny" – *Mamgu* in the South and *Nain* in the North. Annie preferred to be called *Nain* because she thought *Mamgu* made her sound too old!)

<u>**Annie to Beryl.**</u>
Electra House,
Newcastle-Emlyn.
November 4 1941.

My dear Beryl,

How splendid to get the good news, Dad was very excited and came up to Graig Chapel to tell me. I had gone to the prayer meeting.

I feel I want to fly to you and see our little grandson for myself, I hope to be there a little after 1 pm. I do hope they will let me come and see you, as I won't be able to come again until Sunday.

I've been answering the door all day, people giving us congrats and enquiring about you, etc. I'm sure the Queen never had such a lot of congratulations! Keep your chin up – you will soon be home again.

With our fondest love,
        Mother and Dad XXXXX
            and a big hug for Baby.

<u>Beryl to Leonard.</u>   *Maternity Unit,*
                                Carmarthen Infirmary,
                                    Carmarthen.
                                November 6 1941.

Sweetheart Darling,

Just a wee note to tell you how I've been thinking of you all day – your birthday.

I haven't finished knitting your present dear, but have a better gift for you – our little son, who was born on Monday the 3rd about 5.30. He weighed 6½ lbs and is doing well – is very like you, dearest, and has blue eyes. I am managing to feed him, so far.

I am feeling rather tired but the Dr says I'm doing well, and I feel almost myself again, but of course only sleep and rest the whole time.

I came in on Saturday about 1.30 and they gave me induction treatment immediately – castor oil, hot bath, quinine sulphate tablets, 8 injections of pitocin and by 2 am Sunday knew that baby was on his way. Of course, I hoped he would be here sometime Sunday, but things just went on and on till I thought they would never finish. They gave me bromide and brandy to make me have a sleep, but I was very sick, then they tried an injection but I just could not sleep. I went into the labour ward about noon on Monday and thought everything would be over quickly, but was there another six hours.

The sister and midwives were ever so kind and offered me twilight sleep, but as they had said they could tell me the baby's hair was fair, I thought it better not to take any dope as I would be too stupid to obey orders! It just seemed to go on for ever, the most intense pain I have ever experienced.

The Dr would not help me at all, as he said it would be best for me to go on, on my own. I could cheerfully have murdered him at that moment! However, baby was born without instruments and I had no stitches. I had a whiff of chloroform at the very end. So everything went quite straight-forwardly.

So now dearest, do hurry home to see him. I hope to be out one day next week, but will probably have to stay in bed a few days and go quietly afterwards. Wire me c/o Electra House when you arrive, darling.

> *All my love,*
> *Your own Beryl XXXXX*

On November 13 the aircraft carrier *HMS Ark Royal*, one of the most famous warships of WW2, was hit by the German submarine *U-81* near Gibraltar; she capsized and sank the next day. Germany had, for propaganda purposes, repeatedly claimed to have sunk her: this time it was true.

Fred Ball to Beryl.
> *Ravenscourt,*
> *Llandrindod Wells.*
> *November 18 1941.*

Dear Beryl,
I was very pleased indeed to get your letter yesterday morning, and to hear that you and the little man are

progressing favourably. I heard the good news a few hours after the event – I called up Maggie on the phone to ask Gertie to get me a wireless set as mine had gone phut, and she told me that they had phoned Carmarthen about an hour previously, and been told that a fine baby boy had arrived, and that you both were doing well.

A pity we could not get a word to Leonard, as I am sure he must be very anxious. I asked at the post office that same night if I could send a wireless message to him, but they thought not. Well, you gave him a good birthday present this year; now, what would you like me to give the baby? Is there anything special you would like or would you prefer me to give you notes? If the latter, you will have to wait till I come down at Christmas, as I am told I must put them into the baby's own hands (for luck).

What a long time your letter took to get here – I see you posted it on Thursday, and it was only delivered here on Monday morning. I would have answered it last night, but I was called to a fire whilst having tea, so did not get back in time for post.

Well, I'm very glad that everything has gone so well; I've no particular news, so I will close.
With love to you both,
From Dad and <u>Grandad</u> Ball XXXX

On December 7 1941 the Japanese, springing a total surprise, attacked the US naval base at Pearl Harbour in Hawaii. Around 2,400 Americans were killed and 1,200 wounded, and eighteen ships destroyed or run aground. The incident profoundly shocked the American people and demonstrated that they were as vulnerable to attack as any other nation. Previously-strong domestic support for non-intervention disappeared. The following day America declared war on Japan and belatedly entered the conflict in which the rest of the world had already been embroiled for over two years.

<u>Beryl to Leonard.</u>

4 Castle Street,
Newcastle-Emlyn.
January 5 1942.

My Own Darling Husband,

It was so nice to get your letter this morning and to know you had arrived safely, and I do hope this letter will greet you when you reach your next port.

Raymond collected the wireless set on Saturday, and Maggie and the two evacuees came with him, so we had quite a tea party! They came late, as the train was unable to come further than Henllan. Valerie (White Hart) was learning how to work the signals – she is supposed to replace the signal man there – and managed to get a truck across the line! So Maggie had to hire a car from Henllan down. The evacuees had brought baby Clive a pair of gloves and a pair of socks. He is a very lucky boy!

Today I took him to the clinic and he weighed 12lb 2½oz – I don't know if they allowed for his clothes. Anyhow, the Dr seemed very pleased with him, but advised me not to give him the blackcurrant juice and cod-liver oil direct, but to take it myself! I shall have the former, but don't know about the latter!

Kitty has sent Baby a teething ring and a rattle, from the

Isle of Man – the first he has had. Tom and she seem to be settling down nicely there.

We seem to be unlucky about getting your macintosh cleaned. However, if you bring it back with you next time, we'll make a point of getting it done.

Shall be glad to hear from you soon again, dearest. I think of you constantly.

All my love goes with this letter. God bless you, darling.
Your own Beryl XXXX

<u>Beryl to Leonard.</u>

4 Castle Street,
Newcastle-Emlyn.
January 12 1942.

My Darling Husband,
Thank you for your letter received from (censored). It is nice to know you will be home soon again, and Clive and I are both looking forward to seeing you, dear.

You do not say whether you have received my two letters, but perhaps you will get them when you go round to Cardiff.

I am sure (censored) looks quite different from the time when you and I were there together during your "Homeric" days. Does it bring back romantic memories?

Please excuse pencil, dear, but I'm rather tired and can write this way in an easy chair.

Clive frightened himself and his poor mother on Friday. I took several days to get over the shock and still can't bear to think of it. He was crying in his pram and I went to him, turned him over, and patted his back. He still kept on grousing, but I thought he would cry himself to sleep, and my attention was distracted by the coal man who brought coal at that moment. When I went back to have a peep at Baby, he had pulled his cap and the blanket over his face, and was covered with perspiration and as white as a sheet. I thought he had had a fit, but the nurse and Dr both told me it was a "screaming fit" and he had just got into a rage and struggled, and then when the clothes fell over his face, got frightened.

I picked him up every time he cried the next day, and made a pretty little hell for myself. Mother and I could do nothing with him! So we have had to be very firm and let him cry (keeping an eye on him). Now he is as good as gold but we definitely must not nurse him at all as he is getting far too knowing!

Apparently, babies do this sort of thing. Some hold their breath until they are black in the face. One lives and learns! However, it was very frightening being alone in the house when it happened. I put cold hands on his head and he was soon himself and smiling at me, but I was afraid he'd had convulsions. Nurse told me he was all right, and that breast fed babies don't get convulsions.

Well dearest, I'm looking forward ever so much to seeing you again soon. I'm sure you'll find baby Clive has grown. He goes out in his pram every day, and looks very well.

Come home quickly to see us both, dearest.
Your own very loving wife,
Beryl XXXX

From Clive,
XXXX
and hugs.

Winston Churchill said on January 27 1942: "But for the Merchant Navy who bring us the food and munitions of war, Britain would be in a parlous state and indeed, without them, the Army, Navy and Air Force could not operate."

Beryl to Leonard.

*4 Castle Street,
Newcastle-Emlyn.
February 7 1942.*

My Own Dear Husband,

It was so nice to get your letter this morning and to learn you had arrived safely. Ever since you went, I have been looking forward to seeing you again as your stay was so short, and I felt that I had not made as big a fuss of you as I wanted to. However, let us hope you will have more time at home on the next occasion. I have been dreaming of you since you have gone and was so disappointed at not seeing you on waking. You always make me so happy when you are here, dearest.

I went to see Dr Budd yesterday (not having had more than about 4 hours' sleep on Thursday night) and he gave me a good tonic with bromide in it. I already feel better. He told me that if baby Clive did not improve when put down at 6pm, he would give me a sedative for him. Apparently there are some babies that can't relax in the evenings. I didn't ask for a sedative then, as Baby has slept through the evenings since Tuesday night. I had a bit of a tussle with him on Thursday night, and that's what upset my nerves and kept me awake nearly all night, but Baby slept peacefully and is ever so good now.

I have him in the pram in the kitchen all day if I don't go out, and he amuses himself by watching the clock or playing with his hands. He is really most charming, but I don't nurse him except at feeding times.

It will be so nice if he behaves properly next time you come home, darling, as we shall then have much more time together. I am longing to see my dear husband once again. It already seems an eternity since you went, darling, and time passes so slowly when you're away.

Gertie and Cecil are coming down today (so I hear) and I know they will call to get all news.

All my love goes with this letter, sweetheart. God bless you, and keep you. Do come home soon to your little wife and baby.

Your own Beryl XXXX

Leonard to Beryl. *(Ship's name suppressed.)*
February 10 1942.

Cariad Annwyl,

Thank you very much darling for another very nice letter which I received this afternoon. It made me feel very happy, especially the news that little Clive is behaving himself and giving you more rest.

Of course the rest of the letter thrilled me too, cariad. I'm always thrilled when you say you love me, no matter in how many other ways you show it, dear. I love you too, more and more every day, and I'm looking forward now to our next meeting.

Everything is going to plan this time dear, and we should be in the Bristol Channel by Saturday if we take a single stage, or Sunday if it's two stages. If it's Sunday arrival I'm afraid I can't come down till Monday darling, as I'll have to report to Office.

I do hope we'll catch the weekend this time, cariad fach. My leave was so short last time that I couldn't do as much as I wanted to. However, I'll try to make up as soon as we get a decent spell again.

I hope Clive continues with his present behaviour darling. With the better weather coming, you'll both be able to benefit by it then. The worst of the winter is over now, and later on, when summer arrives, you'll be able to go to the seaside; and of course, when I'm home I'll be able to come too.

I'm feeling fine and very fit, but am missing you both very much.

> *Lots and lots of love to both,*
> *Your very loving husband*
> *Leonard XXXX*

<u>Leonard to Beryl.</u> (Ship's name suppressed.)
February 15 1942.

My Little Sweetheart,

Another opportunity of writing to let you know that I'm quite safe and well, and thinking of you both very much indeed, has occurred, dearest. This is the second letter I'm writing from here, so things are going well in the correspondence line this voyage.

I haven't received any mail from you yet cariad, but perhaps it's a bit early to expect any. I'm anxious to know how you are both keeping, whether your cold is better and whether little Clive is well again. I do hope you are both picking up now and getting over it nicely.

Torpedoed Dreams

We have a new Captain here at the moment. He is relieving Captain Davies for the voyage. Captain Davies's son who was in the RAF is reported missing, which is very sad especially as Mrs Davies's health is so poor. Captain Davies thought it best to stay with her until they can get some definite news.

Things are much better this time to what they were last voyage, dear, especially in the cooking line. You need not worry about me at all in that direction, sweetheart. Of course, it isn't up to the standard of home cooking at all and I'm just as homesick as I've ever been, but it will do until our next spot of leave.

You can't imagine how much I'm looking forward to seeing you again, cariad. Time seems to pass so slowly here. I think of you both for hours and hours, wondering how you are and what you are doing, and wishing like anything that I were with you to share in it all. You can't realise, dear, how much I look forward to the end of this war, to getting a shore job and being with you at home for always.

I hope it won't be very long before that happy day is with us, darling. I hope I can sit my exam this year so as to help us along. Every step in that direction will cheer us both I'm sure, dear, and I've tried hard enough to deserve some reward now.

Won't it be nice when we can get our reward, cariad. When I can be home with you always and share in your lives as I'm longing so much to do at present. I've spent quite enough time wandering around the world now. Whatever they write in story books about the adventure and "call of the sea", I know one person who is quite prepared to become stone deaf to it all.

I know too, dear, that short spells of home comfort beat all the adventure one can get out of visiting foreign ports. If these are examples of what the future holds for me at home, (and there's no reason why they shouldn't be), then roll on the day when I pack my bag and leave the sea for good. You and little Clive are everything in the world to me. All my thoughts and all my ambitions centre around you two. I want to make you both very happy. I want to repay you for the hours of happiness you have brought to me, but until I get ashore for good I can't possibly hope to do that, sweetheart.

Do you remember, during the darkest days of this war, how Churchill called to the people and ended with these words: "But to the West, the land is bright." We too must look to the future, for that is also bright darling. Haven't I, thanks to your help, emerged from one terrible cloud of depression (those days when I was on the tanker) and haven't we done well since then, dear? We can do better than that when this war is over, so cheer up cariad and look forward to it all.

I hope to get a few more letters posted later on, dearest. I'm looking forward too, to receiving news from you shortly. I don't know whether there is a long delay between my posting and your receiving my letters, but you can write for at least another ten days after the date I gave you when I left.

Lots and lots of love to you both. I'm always thinking of you, dear.

> *Your very loving*
> *Leonard and Daddy*
> *XXXX*

<u>Beryl to Leonard.</u>

4 Castle Street,
Newcastle-Emlyn.
March 4 1942.

Sweetheart,

Just a note to greet you on arrival, as usual.

Thanks ever so much for the apples, to hand today. They are really delicious. It was so good of you to send them. I gave Maggie four, as she would not take anything else. Apparently, Mr Swete should have plenty of fruit for his complaint, but can't always get it. That's why I made Maggie take some.

She was charmed with baby Clive, who was on his very best behaviour. It has been such a glorious day. Mother, Maggie, Baby and I went for a walk along the Llandyfriog road, and Maggie caught the bus there.

Baby has been naughty this evening, though. I think he got a bit over-excited today. You know how he gets – just can't relax. However, he has gone to sleep now.

Leonard darling, we miss you so much. Every time you go, the heartache gets worse and worse. You were so very sweet to me again this time. I appreciate it doubly now, at a time when I need all your sympathy and help, and don't feel up to the mark. No wonder I love you! You are always such a good husband. I hope to be able to repay all your kindness one day.

A receipt arrived this morning for your entrance fee for the C&G Exam. I dare say the rest of the particulars will follow.

Mother and I gathered a big bunch of snowdrops today. I'm glad the spring is nearly with us as I'm so tired of the bleak wintry weather.

*I'll write again soon. All my love, darling, and thanks
again for all your kindness.*
    Your own
      Beryl XXXX

Fred to Beryl.
                                    *Ravenscourt,
Llandrindod Wells.
March 5 1942.*

Dear Beryl and Clive,

*It was such a delightful surprise to receive your letter last
Monday. You know, I like getting letters but I'm a terrible bad
one to write them; I suppose that's a failing with others of the
family which I suppose must be put down to heredity. I get
about one letter every three weeks from Llandysul. I must
say, Raymond is very good: I get one every Monday from him
and I write him every fortnight, just a scribble in pencil for
writing is my bugbear!*

*I'm very pleased to hear of the progress made by His
Lordship; poor Beryl, you must have had a shock, but what a
relief to find your fears unfounded. I can quite understand
how you must have felt, and how it tended you to start a bad
habit; you know, being too kind is as great a fault as not
being kind enough. Leonard, Gertie and Raymond never got
too much attention as Mother was too busy in the bakehouse.
Maggie did most of the spoiling, if they <u>were</u> spoilt (that's a
matter of opinion!).*

*Did you see in the paper that Llandrindod Wells won the
first prize of £500 in the Waste Paper salvage campaign for
the district of south Wales and Herefordshire? We collected
29.37 lbs per head of population – the largest figure for the*

whole of the country! Cardigan is third (£100) and Carmarthen shares one of the three £50 prizes. Tomorrow night at the Grand Pavilion the chairman of the Council is being presented with the cheque for £500. I have a reserved balcony ticket for the pictures and the presentation from the Council in recognition of my help in the matter (all who helped in any way have had the same.)

It must be nice to have Leonard popping in and out so frequently. I do hope he will now be able to get his City and Guilds.

Well, I think I've about come to the end of my news so I'll close, with love from
Dad and Grandad Ball XXXX

Beryl to Leonard.

4 Castle Street,
Newcastle-Emlyn.
March 6 1942.

Cariad,
Do please excuse this writing paper, but it is all I can find at the moment. I meant to have written last night, but was rather sick (I ate some stew which was too rich), so did not feel like doing anything much after putting Baby to bed.

The snaps have not come yet but I'll enquire again tomorrow.

Baby Clive has been a bit grousy these last two days. I expect my tummy being upset has upset him too. I shan't be sorry when I finish feeding him as if I get upset, I get a double dose of it – grousy baby as well!

He has discovered he can make the most delicious gargling noises and we are favoured with these when he feels full of fun, bless him!

I paid for the coat yesterday – they charged £4/12/6 for cash and gave me 1/- back, so it really cost £4/11/6. Thanks again and again for your lovely present, darling.

The weather is simply horrible after the sudden burst of spring on Wednesday. I awoke to find snow on the ground this morning and felt very cold and shivery. However, we had brilliant sunshine this afternoon although the wind was still keen.

Dad has had a wire to say his sister is very ill. I expect he will go to see her at Ipswich this weekend. Poor Dad, he seems to be having a lot of family troubles these last few months.

It was nice to get your note from Barry, dearest – it cheered me up no end. I love you too, beloved, more and more each day. Do come home quickly. It makes such a difference when you are here: life is so monotonous without you.

The WI Eisteddfod is tonight, but I don't feel like going. Mother has gone to collect the prizes (!!). I entered a knitted baby's dress, but there are one or two mistakes in it!

Goodnight dearest. May God bless and keep you.

Your own

Beryl XXXX

Leonard to Beryl. *(Ship's name suppressed.)*

March 24 1942.

My dearest,

Thank you lots and lots for the nice letter, which I have just received, cariad. I hope you were not counting on a letter before we left, dear. You see, I didn't get aboard until midnight and we were at sea when I was called next morning.

We've had some very cold weather here too, darling. On Saturday we actually had snow, and as we were not very far from your vicinity I wondered whether you had had any as well. In a way I was glad that I didn't plant the patch I had dug in the garden as we had frost last night and the night before.

Perhaps little Clive is cutting his eye teeth first after all, darling. If so, he's behaving very well indeed, as I believe the eye teeth are the most difficult of all. Of course, I don't know much about these things, but it would account for his eyes being sore, wouldn't it?

Thank you very much for all the love which you express so nicely in your letter. I love you too my darling, from the very bottom of my heart, and I'm looking forward to being home again. You see, dearest, no matter how much I love you I can't express it on paper as intensely as I want to. It's simply not possible to put into words the longing and yearning that is in my heart for you, beloved; nor is it possible to describe the great joy that is mine because of the knowledge that you are my little wife and that you love me, dear.

The happiest years of my life have been those during which we have loved each other, sweetheart. Baby Clive has come now to increase that happiness, and it only needs peace in the world and a shore job to make my happiness complete.

Lots and lots of love to both of you,
Your very loving husband and Daddy,
Leonard XXXX

<u>Leonard to Beryl.</u>

(Ship's name suppressed.)
April 29 1942.

Cariad Annwyl,

Just a few lines again today to tell you how much I am missing you, dear. Already I am looking forward eagerly to our return and to our next leave together.

I haven't forgotten to post the bag on to you dearest. I have it packed ready and will forward it the same time as this letter. I hope you'll have some nice weather and that you and little Clive will have some nice times by the sea.

And when I'm next home I can join you and make it even more enjoyable for you darling. I wonder whether we'll be able to hold Clive's feet in the water and whether he'll like it? Anyway I'm sure we'll have lots of nice times there.

I'm sorry I didn't finish the garden, cariad, but I hope you'll be able to get it done. Perhaps Uncle Johnny could give you an afternoon. The heavy work is finished and he could do the planting nicely.

I shan't be writing again before we leave, dearest, but you know I love you from the bottom of my heart. I'm looking forward to seeing you again, cariad. Keep your little chin up always my dear, and think of the nice times we'll have when I return. Little Clive will have changed a bit by then and who knows, he might be able to say "Dad" or "Mam". Personally, I hope it's the latter.

May God bless you both and keep you well and safe always.

Lots and lots of love and kisses,
Your very very loving husband
Leonard XXXX

<u>Leonard to Beryl.</u>

(Ship's name suppressed.)
August 30 1942.

My Little Sweetheart,

We've arrived safely in this place, cariad, and I wish it were possible for me to ship home for a few hours just to thank you for the lovely time I spent with you both.

I have thought of you constantly since leaving, darling, and it's quite true that the longer my leave, the harder it is to settle down again to life on board.

I've missed you and baby Clive more than I can describe, sweetheart. It seemed quite strange not to wake up and greet you with a good morning kiss and feel tiny hands grabbing at my face, and hear childish laughter in my ears.

I'm looking forward to it when I return, and hope we'll be home very quickly. When I'm next home I hope to have some toys for Clive to play with. I wonder how much he'll change between now and then, dearest.

Diolch yn fawr iawn am yr amser rhagorol ces i gyda ti, cariad. Rwy'n dy garu di'n fwy nag erioed. Byddaf i'n meddwl amdanat ti yr oll amser, ac yn edrych ymlaen am y tro nesa'.

I love you with all my heart dearest. You and baby Clive have made me very happy, far happier than I can explain in words.

Love me always dearest like you do now, and may God bless you both and keep you safe always.

Your very loving husband,
Leonard
XXXX

Leonard (left) on an unidentified ship during the War.

<u>Leonard to Beryl.</u> *(Ship's name suppressed.)*
October 12 1942.

My Little Sweetheart,

I'm sorry I won't be home to greet you personally on your birthday, darling, but I hope this letter will be in time to convey my very best wishes with all the love that is in my heart. Many Happy Returns of the Day, beloved, and may you have many more birthdays, birthdays that I can share with you in person. I've bought you a lovely box of chocolates and three pairs of silk stockings for a present, and hope it won't be long before I'm able to give them to you.

How I wish I were home with you, cariad fach. Somehow

or other we always manage to be apart on these occasions. Only last weekend I was telling Reynolds (my friend at the last place) of the flowers I bought you one year, and of how long they had lasted under your loving care. Flowers won't last half as long as that out here.

For Clive's birthday I've got a lovely Teddy Bear. I'm sure he'll like it dear, but I doubt whether I'll be quite in time to give it to him on the appropriate date. His birthday is a little too far ahead yet to be very definite, but I think we'll just miss it.

You'll have one consolation darling. This will be your first birthday that Clive will be able to share with you. He'll be too young, of course, to understand what it's all about but in future years he'll be able to help to make it really happy for you, dear. He'll be looking forward to this time of the year, I think. First your birthday, then his own and then mine. Life will be one round of parties and I bet he'll enjoy himself!

We too have a lot to look forward to, sweetheart. When this war is over and I get that shore job there'll be much more in life for us. We've got little Clive to bring up, and that alone should become more interesting every day now. When he's quite old enough to look after himself you'll feel less tied darling, so on this birthday don't feel you're getting any older, but look forward to the future and all its prospects.

I love you more today than I've ever loved you dear, and all your future birthdays will find my love stronger than the previous ones.

Lots and lots of love, dear. God bless you both,
Your very loving husband,
Leonard XXXX

<u>Beryl to Leonard.</u>

4 Castle Street,
Newcastle-Emlyn.
November 12 1942.

Cariad Annwyl,

Just a wee note to thank you very much indeed for your two most welcome letters to hand. What a pity the phoning is so difficult! But now I'm looking forward to seeing you, and so is Clive, who sends kisses and hugs in return for the special kisses you sent him.

The Teddy Bear has not arrived yet, but I will of course do as you ask, dearest. We went to tea at the Vicarage yesterday. Pauline came too, and both babies behaved themselves remarkably well.

Clive is nearly walking on his own, but can only balance a few steps. You shall teach him to go properly!Cariad, the weekend seems a long·way off. However I must be patientand hope the intervening time will pass quickly.

Need I say: "I love you, sweetheart" – but I'll repeat the familiar though sweet saying.

Rwy'n dy garu - tyrd adre'n gloi.
Your own
Beryl XXXX

Another addition to the family came on April 3 1943 when my cousin Celia was born in Carmarthen to Gertie and Cecil. Cecil was in the Army, and had recently been posted to India.

A Dance with the Duchess

According to the *Manifest of Alien Passengers,* Leonard entered New York on HMS *Queen Mary* on May 11 1943, listed with nine others on a group transit visa. They were on their way to be members of the crew of s/s *Jesse G Cotting,* later renamed the *Trostan,* built on the Great Lakes for Britain under the Emergency Shipbuilding Program, and were to depart from Sturgeon Bay, Wisconsin on the new ship for the Atlantic convoys later that month.

Photo: Wikipedia, Public Domain.

HMS *Queen Mary* in New York in her wartime grey paint.

Winston Churchill was on the same voyage of the *Queen Mary,* travelling under the alias of Colonel Warden, to meet President Roosevelt and to attend the TRIDENT conference, when the British and Americans reached an agreement to mount a cross-Channel invasion, later called *Operation Overlord*, with a target date of May 1 1944. (The reason for the year-long delay was the need to build up allied troop strength, landing craft, and supplies, and the D-day landings actually took place on June 6 1944.)

The *Queen Mary* was also carrying 5,000 German prisoners of war.

<u>Leonard to Beryl.</u>   *New York.*
                                                               May 16 1943.

Cariad Annwyl,

It is Sunday afternoon and I'm sitting in Central Park writing this letter.

There are crowds of people around. Men and women in uniform, courting couples trying to make the most of their time together, older people enjoying their walk and the spring air and of course, myself, trying to think of a really nice way to express my love to you. You see, darling, I'm really having a wonderful time here and I ought to appreciate it all, but in my heart I'm feeling very lonely and wishing more every day that I could share just a few of my experiences with you.

I can't tell you anything now about the voyage as it will probably go down in history as a great occasion and censorship will be very strict, but I can of course write about events since my arrival here.

I'm staying at a first class hotel right in the centre of the city, and only one block away from Broadway. I'm very comfortable there, having a bedroom to myself with a bathroom attached. The food is excellent, and the management are most helpful with assisting us to find our way around.

There are clubs and parties for men in Uniform. Some set up by our own people here, and others by local voluntary institutions. There are lunches and dinners and dances in plenty and one shouldn't really be bored for one minute.

I've been round quite a lot of them, and on Friday night at the British Merchant Officers' Club I met the Duke of Windsor and danced with the Duchess! I hadn't really bargained for that; I knew they were coming, of course, and I went along to see them, as I thought. You can imagine then, dearest, how nervous I felt when I discovered that I was the senior member present in my own department, and as such had to represent them.

I shook hands with the Duke and Duchess and stammered a few words of greeting, which my friends said afterwards were very nice, but I think I'd have been happier really if the ground had opened suddenly and swallowed me up! Later in the evening the Duke and Duchess joined in a Paul Jones, and it was here that I got my dance with the Duchess.

But all this is by the way. All my enjoyment is really artificial so long as I am parted from you and Clive, darling. You see, dear, it's like the sour grapes story. I'd simply love to have an opportunity to take you around here with me. If we could have just a week of it together it would be marvellous.

We'd have the time of our lives together, but I can't really enjoy it because the little woman I love, and my one permanent partner in this world, isn't here.

Without you it all seems so empty, and though I could stay away and perhaps not feel quite so discontented about it, I should probably be just as miserable in my rooms for the sake of having something to do.

Every day my love for you grows greater and greater. I have seen and done nothing here yet that I wouldn't exchange for just one hour with you, cariad. You are always in my thoughts, and when I'm enjoying myself I'm unhappy because I'm not enjoying myself with you.

It's an awful mixture isn't it, dearest? – the body going one way and the heart pulling the other way. You have my heart for ever beloved and no matter where I am or what I do that is always with you and in your keeping.

This morning I went to St George's church in Greenwich Village and really enjoyed the service. Dr Reinell (I think that was his name) from Yale University preached a wonderful sermon on "What does it profit a man if he gains the whole world and thereby loses his soul?" The church was packed and the singing was beautiful, and once again I was homesick because I wished you could have been with me, dear.

I'm afraid this state of affairs will last for five or six weeks yet – that is the best news I can gather at the moment. I'll write regularly and often sweetheart, but I'm going to miss you like H---. I'm missing you more now than I've ever missed you. I feel like swearing because we could have such a grand time together, whereas now it seems such an awful waste.

Lots and lots of love darling, and a big hug and kiss for Clive from Daddy. May God bless and keep you both safe.

Your very very loving husband,
Leonard XXXX

<u>Leonard to Beryl.</u>

New York.
June 3 1943.

Cariad Annwyl,

Just a few lines again today to let you know how much I am thinking of you and missing you, sweetheart. Time seems to pass very slowly these days and I find myself thinking of you and Clive and home, missing you all more and more every day.

Actually I ought to be very contented and happy over here. The people are exceptionally kind and do their utmost to make us feel at home. There are lots of clubs open to us, sightseeing tours arranged for us, dances and theatres and the movies, all free of charge. One can find something to do for 24 hours every day and yet, in spite of it all, I'm getting very bored.

You see, dearest, there is nothing here that my heart yearns for. My little wife, and son, and home. Wherever I go and whatever I do, I'm always thinking of you and wishing like H--- that you were with me, cariad. Spending my time like this seems so empty, dear. I don't really enjoy myself because my heart is always at home with you. Music, dancing, theatres, cafés or a trip to the country all remind me of days we have spent together in the past darling and I am constantly asking myself the question: "Why must I be here with these people? Why, oh why can't I spend these hours with the two little dears that I love more than anything else in the world?" How much nicer it would be sweetheart if, instead of sunbathing on the beach at Coney Island, I were making sand castles for Clive at Aberporth. If, instead of guiding quite charming hostesses around the dance floor at one of the clubs, I were dancing with you, sweetheart.

And how nice it would be to receive a letter from you, cariad. I know you have no address to write to, and I can't give you one yet, but my heart does long to hear from you.

I'm homesick and very love sick, cariad annwyl. No matter how hard I try I shall never be able to explain properly how great is the ache where my heart should be, or how very much I love you. I'm looking forward eagerly to our next meeting and am simply longing to hold you and little Clive in my arms again.

What makes it worse, dearest, is that there is still no news of when we are likely to leave. Shall we make a date for August Bank Holiday, because I'd like to take you to the seaside then, and if my future letters do not change it, I shall be with you reasonably near that day. Our June luck seems to have gone all wrong this year, my darling. June has such a lot of very pleasant memories that it is no wonder at all why I'm so particularly love sick now, is it?

Love me always cariad fach, because you mean so very much to me.

May God bless you both and keep you safe always.
Your very loving, very love sick husband
Leonard. XXXX

Time dragged on and on. The *Jesse G Cotting* eventually sailed from Superior, Wisconsin on July 10 1943, and reached Montreal on the 24th. For a new ship, her reliability was very questionable! Unspecified repairs were expected to keep her and her crew there until August 8, but ran over time and she was detained until the 14th.

<u>Leonard to Beryl.</u>

Montreal.
August 8 1943.

My Own Darling Wife,
    Another Sunday is passing, reminding me that time marches on, in spite of my terrible impatience and the feeling that it hasn't moved very quickly since we were last together.

    I'm still feeling very, very lovesick and am filled with longing for your sweet company, cariad. All day I've been thinking of you, dear, wishing I could take you in my arms and nearly smother you with kisses. You can't imagine how much I am missing you, sweetheart; there seems to be a big empty space where my heart should be, not really empty when it aches so badly, but an awful numbness that I know I'll have to endure until we meet again.

    Yesterday too, sweetheart I felt exactly the same. I woke up thinking of you, and all the morning I couldn't settle down to doing any work, though there was plenty to be done. Then in the afternoon I had a brainwave. I thought I'd do something for you, dear, and I started making you an ironing board. I found some wood and borrowed some tools and spent one of the happiest afternoons I've had since I left home. I've made a really good job of it, considering the material I had at my disposal, and I do hope you'll like it because it is a product of my love for you - you know, something I did for you because for once I wanted to be practical about my love for you. It just didn't seem right just to sit down and say: "Well I'm in love, I'm very lonely, and my little wife is much too far away to dispel that longing and yearning that has been gnawing at my heart for such a very long time now". Instead, sweetheart, I felt I had to do something for you, hence the ironing board.

Now I am wondering what I shall make you next. I expect I'll think of something else you need before we leave here, which I hope and pray will not be very long now, dear.

Are you missing me too, my sweet? I know you are, cariad, and I wish very much that I could do something about that. I've written you lots and lots of nice letters; some of them very long and very loving, others just short notes, but still with lots of love in them. I wish I could receive just one letter from you now, dear – it would cheer me up no end.

Do you know, sweetheart, this is the first summer since our engagement that we haven't been able to spend a little of it together. It will be autumn before I shall be home now, but it should still be warm enough for us to spend a few days by the sea.

Have you managed to get to the beach fairly often dearest? And does Clive enjoy himself thoroughly there? I'm just longing to give him his tricycle, and he ought to have lots of fun with it at the front of the house – that concrete pavement will be just the thing if we can keep the little rascal within its boundary!

I wonder how much he has grown since I've been away this time. I don't suppose I'll find him growing so very much in future, but I expect I'll find lots of progress in other directions. How much does he talk now? Does he still look at my photograph and say "Dad-dad"? Is he a greater comfort to you now, darling? I mean, can you leave him a little more to play on his own when you are busy and then find him great company when you have time to play with him?

Cariad fach, I do so want to see you both now. I feel so very homesick tonight and I'm missing you both more than I can possibly describe on paper. My heart is overflowing with love for you, and my whole being hungry to be near you. I'm longing so very much to hear you say you love me, darling, even though you have told me so hundreds of times.

I'd like to take you for a nice walk in the country tonight, beloved. We could walk along the road to Cwm Valley, arm in arm together, and speak of our love for eachother. We could sit awhile among the bracken and I could take you in my arms and kiss your sweet lips, darling. I could look at you - at your beautiful dark hair and your lovely eyes, and drink thirstily from the fountain of love light that I see reflected there. I could hold you close to me and tell you, much more beautifully than I can on paper, just how very much I love you.

When I come home this time, sweetheart, we'll have to try and arrange to go out a few evenings like that. You know, just as we used to during our courting days. I still want to take you out courting even though we've been married so long. I'm much more in love with you today than I was a few years ago, and I know it will always keep on growing.

Look forward to lots and lots of love and affection when I return, my dear. It won't be so very long now, so keep your little chin up for just a little while more. For the present, darling, be comforted by the knowledge that I love you very, very much indeed.

Lots of love to both,
Your very loving husband,
Leonard XXXX

The *Jesse G Cotting* arrived in Quebec on August 15 1943.

After she sailed again, her unreliability continued. Boiler defects were reported and the vessel was towed back to Quebec for repairs on the 18th. She eventually left Quebec on September 3, arrived in Chatham, New Brunswick on the 5th, and Sydney, Nova Scotia on the 14th. The next day she set off across the Atlantic and arrived safely in the port of Sharpness, Gloucestershire, on September 30. At last Leonard was able to have almost a month's holiday at home!

The next ship Leonard joined was the *Nyanza*. She sailed from Cardiff on November 3 1943, my second birthday, and called at Milford Haven on the 4th. The Admiralty records show that she was chartered for "Army Collier service to the Mediterranean". This was a voyage where the vessel and her crew were incredibly lucky to escape unharmed; Leonard of course could not write about the events, but thanks to the National Archives I've been able to trace what happened.

<u>Leonard to Beryl.</u> *(Ship's name suppressed.)*
November 4 1943.

Cariad,

I have been thinking of you and Clive all through my watch, dearest. It is nearly 7 am now and I was just thinking how nice it would be if I could bring you a cup of tea and kiss you good morning, or just wake up and find you standing by the bed with a cup of tea for me. I've missed you both such a terrible lot since Monday that already I'm looking forward to coming home again.

Yesterday I celebrated our little one's birthday here all on my own. When afternoon tea came up I cut the cake and imagined I was home with you, cariad. The cake was really delicious and I'm afraid I made an awful pig of myself by eating nearly half of it! The rest I shall keep until Saturday.

I'm very satisfied with my new ship, darling. There's a very good crowd of Officers aboard and plenty of good food. Those who were here last voyage speak well of her, and of course being three to do the watches makes a very big difference. I'll be able to concentrate more on studying now.

But in spite of this satisfaction, my dear, I wish my leave were just starting over again. The one I've just spent with you was one of the happiest we've had together darling. You were so very very nice to me and I honestly can't find the words to express my thanks for all you did.

Our third mate seems to know quite a lot about your family. He knows your uncles Benny and Johnny and "Oil Jenkins Bach". He knows your mother, too, but not as well as he knows the men in her family. When you see uncle Johnny please give him his best regards.*

Well cariad fach, here am I just gossiping now and it's nearly breakfast time. I haven't yet said how much I love you, but you know that without my saying so. Every day my love grows and grows and you can't imagine how much I'm looking forward to the time when we can be together always.

* "Jenkins Bach" was Beryl's maternal grandfather, who was renowned as a herbalist, and his "Oil" was famed in the district as a cure for boils, whitlows and other kinds of inflammation. During the War, Winston Churchill was reported to be suffering from boils, and Beryl's Uncle Johnny sent him a bottle of the oil to treat them. He received a polite letter from Churchill's secretary thanking him for his concern. It didn't say whether Churchill had actually used the oil!

Thank you once again, dear, for a very nice leave and for all you have done for me. I appreciate it all very much, and one day will try to repay you in the way I feel you deserve to be repaid.

Give Clive a big hug and kiss from me and tell him to give Mummy a big big kiss for Daddy.

Lots and lots of love to you both, and may God bless and keep you always.

Your very, very loving husband
Leonard XXXX

A Narrow Escape

The Admiralty records show that the *Nyanza* entered the Mediterranean and arrived at Augusta, Sicily (which was in Allied hands) on November 26, departing the same day. Two days later she was in Brindisi. She was bound for Bari, but due to the immense congestion of shipping in that port, anchored in Brindisi to wait her turn – a fortuitous delay. A horrendous event occurred while she was there.

During the Italian campaign in 1943, the port of Bari (about 60 miles northwest of Brindisi) was an important supply point for Allied forces. Crucial supplies and provisions were unloaded there from ships and transported to the Allies, who were attempting to push the Germans northwards out of the Italian peninsula.

On the evening of December 2 the German *Luftwaffe*, achieving complete surprise, launched a massive attack on Allied forces and shipping in Bari harbour, which was brightly lit. 27 cargo and transport ships and a schooner were sunk, and 12 others damaged. Two ammunition ships exploded, shattering windows seven miles away, and rupturing a bulk petrol pipe line. The gushing fuel ignited and a burning sheet spread over the water, engulfing otherwise undamaged ships.

Horrifyingly, mustard gas was released from one of the destroyed American cargo ships, the *John Harvey*, and added considerably to the total loss of life of nearly 2,000 mercantile marine, military and civilian personnel. (The gas was being transported to Europe to be kept for retaliation in case Hitler used chemical weapons: both British and US governments covered this up for years afterwards.) The attack, called the "Little Pearl Harbour", put the port of Bari out of action for a couple of weeks and it only became fully operational again in February 1944.

Eventually the *Nyanza* moved from Brindisi to what was left of Bari on December 17 1943 and unloaded her cargo. She remained there until December 30 then steamed back through the Mediterranean via Augusta and Gibraltar and set course for Ghana in Africa.

<u>Leonard to Beryl.</u>   (From records: *Takoradi, Ghana.*)
Feb 10 1944.

Cariad,

It won't be very long now before we are together again, sweetheart. We're on the last stage of this long voyage and already I'm feeling very excited about the prospect of seeing you soon. We may be delayed a little on the way, but not by more than two or three weeks.

I've already told you in my letters, dear, how much I've been missing you these last few months, and as our next leave together grows nearer I keep missing you more and more. Your nice letters have helped to cheer me up, but of course, no matter how nicely you express your love in them, I still feel very lonely and long to be with you again.

I've been very busy these last few days putting the finishing touches to Clive's "Puffer Train." It's not a bad job really, but the facilities for doing a really good job are very poor and it's not half as ambitious a model as I would have liked it to be. However, I couldn't possibly turn up without one and perhaps it will be better if I put off making a really good model until he's a little older.

It's very hot out here darling, and I'm getting quite a good tan. I'm sorry you haven't more sun at home, but believe me, we'd give anything for a good cold frosty day at the moment! Isn't it a pity that we can't somehow compromise in the matter – me send you huge armfuls of this very hot sunshine, and you send me some of the miserable cold.

Cariad fach, rwy'n hiraethu ar dy ôl yn ofnadwy. Lately I've been feeling very homesick and lovesick. This morning I was in the water swimming and I thought of those lovely times we spent together at Aberporth when we were courting, and of last summer when we managed just one day on the beach with little Clive. This year I hope we'll be able to have a few days by the sea together.

Would you please send in my name for the examination in Radio Communication Grade 2; I'm studying very hard these days and have every confidence of passing. We'll be home in time for me to make whatever arrangements are necessary should I have to sail again before the date of the exam. I'm getting very anxious to have it over now as I don't care very much for studying the same subjects over and over again.

One day I hope to repay you for all the love and devotion you have shown me during these years of constant parting. I'm just longing and longing for the time when we can be together always.

Look forward to seeing me soon, cariad. For the present, lots and lots of love and kisses to you both.

May God bless you always,
Your loving husband
Leonard XXXX

<u>Beryl to Leonard.</u>

4 Castle Street,
Newcastle-Emlyn.
February 13 1944.

Cariad,

Just another love letter to cheer you up, wherever you are. We are so much longing to see you again, dear.

Clive is picking up rapidly on "Parrish's Food" and I had a good night's sleep last night – the first for 3 weeks. He had got into the habit of waking up and was so cold that I had to take him into bed to get him warm. I naturally didn't want the habit to persist! He has been arranging snowdrops and daffodils in vases for me these last few days, and does them very nicely. The living room is beginning to look quite homely again now that Clive takes a pride in keeping the flowers tidy. Mother has given me two old-fashioned china dogs to put on the mantelpiece.

Kitty came down to see us last Wednesday. She is terribly thin and needs a good rest. I would so like her to come and stay here, but Barbara wakes so very early (about 5.30 some mornings) that I could not manage between Clive and her.

Cecil has managed to get into his own trade in the Army and is doing a course in electrical work. Gertie looks very well now. Your Dad has had a slight rupture – as you know, he will overdo things.

Leonard dear, it will be so nice to have you home again: it is scarcely a home here without you, and if I didn't have Clive it would be just a house – but we are very fortunate to have that in wartime.

Clive sings hymns quite well now. Mother has been singing "Nearer my God to Thee" and I get snatches of this, in a mournful minor key, every few minutes!

You know how much I love and long for you, darling. It should be lovely spring weather when you arrive. Clive is writing these kisses himself XXXX and sends heaps of love and so do I. God bless you, beloved,
Beryl XXXX

The first paragraph of the next letter presumably refers to the events at Bari:

Beryl to Leonard.   *4 Castle Street,*
Newcastle-Emlyn.

February 24 1944.

Cariad,
It was so good of the Owners to write me the other day to say you were safe and well, or rather, that the ship had arrived safely in a foreign port and all aboard were safe. I only hope this unexpected communication from the Owners doesn't mean that you've been involved in any excitement. I suppose it does mean, however, that you'll be longer away from home than you at first thought.

I've been longing so much to see you, lately, dear. It seems ages since you were with us. Clive looks at your photo very often and talks to it. How we are both longing to see you again! So long as you are safe and well, we must try to be patient, although it's very hard at times.

We had such a lovely day at Llandysul yesterday. Kitty and Barbara came too, but Mother couldn't manage it at the last minute. (Kitty and Barbara are staying with her.)

Clive does love having Barbara over to play with him. His appetite has improved a lot since she started coming to have dinner with him. They fight quite a lot and I have to be referee, but I think they are settling down quite well. Barbara wants all Clive's toys and he is very unselfish and gives in to her. On the other hand, he is a dreadful tease (like his Daddy) and runs after her holding the cat in front of him (she hates cats!). Also he pushes her, which she detests. He generally gives her a push and then "loves" her to make it up!

Oh, I nearly forgot a very important piece of news. Rayda and I have rented a bungalow at Tresaith for the month of June. It worked out at £6-15-0 each for the month, and there will be room for you to squeeze in if you happen to be home on leave, dear. Mother and (Rayda's husband) Jack hope to come for a short time too, so you see it is really a very inexpensive holiday. We have paid in advance so as to be sure of having it. I must try to save up now to cover the cheque!

Cariad, I do long to see you once again. You know how I love you, dear. Life is so happy when you are here. Come home soon. God bless you,
Your own Beryl XXXX

Leonard was hoping to be home for three weeks over Easter 1944. The National Archives records show that the *Nyanza* sailed from Freetown, Sierra Leone on February 21, reaching the Clyde Anchorage on March 13. She then moved to Greenock for the 14th and 15th, was diverted to Glasgow from the 15th to the 19th, to Workington on the 21st, then back to Glasgow on the 23rd. Poor Leonard saw his leave fast disappearing around the Clyde; little wonder that he was rather despondent: his voyage over, yet unable to join his family. He was eventually paid off, and reached Newcastle-Emlyn on March 28.

<u>Leonard to Beryl.</u>   *Glasgow.*
March 24 1944.

Cariad Annwyl,

It was nice to hear you on the telephone last night dear, though the line was pretty hopeless. I had such a lot to say to you but couldn't owing to the difficulty of hearing each other.

I expect to be home about next Monday or Tuesday. If we are very lucky it may be Sunday but I don't think so now. We've been messed about such a lot these last few days that I'm feeling positively fed up and very disappointed with everything, dear.

I'm glad the bananas arrived in good condition. I made a very special effort to get them home nicely and nursed them very tenderly!

Thank you, darling, for arranging the examination details. I've made enquiries in Glasgow concerning the procedure and it depends now on what I'm doing when we get to Glasgow again. I don't think there'll be any difficulty about my sitting it this year, and I'll be able to sit it before I leave if I know there's no possible chance of my being back in time to sit under ordinary procedure. I can't arrange anything just yet though because I don't know what we're doing; whether we're paying off or what. That will be decided over the weekend.

My darling, it seems much too long to wait until early next week before I see you. I've been longing and longing all the voyage to be with you dear and now that I've heard your sweet voice again, that longing has grown a hundred fold. (Remainder missing).

I remember the bananas – they were unobtainable during the war, and a great treat. Leonard posted them from Scotland as soon as he arrived. The big bunch hung in the kitchen for some time to ripen fully. I wondered why the bananas had come but not Daddy.

Beryl, Leonard and me in the garden at 4 Castle Street, April 1944.

By now, I was becoming increasingly aware and remembering things, but "Daddy" was a mysterious someone beyond my recall. Beryl spoke so lovingly about him I knew he had to be nice. And so he proved to be. I sat between them when he brought a tea tray to bed in the mornings, and loved cuddling him, being lifted high in the air, climbing on him and investigating his jacket pockets. One day I fell head-first into a bush when watching him working in the garden. He roared with laughter, which bruised my dignity. My loss of face was compounded because my nappy needed changing! But he soon lifted me out, with a reassuring cuddle.

Another bitter disappointment awaited Leonard and Beryl: he was assigned to the s/s *Shahzada* and would have to leave again on April 6 – the day before Good Friday – to travel to Glasgow, and so would not even have Easter at home as they'd anticipated. Fate seemed determined to give them as little time together as possible.

On the 6th Beryl and I went to see Leonard off again. Gracie Fields was singing *Wish Me Luck As You Wave Me Goodbye* on the radio as we left the house. I rode on his shoulders, feeling very proud and important.

We stopped at *Electra House* for Annie and Jack to say their farewells, then walked the 200 yards or so up Sycamore Street to where the red Western Welsh bus was waiting near the Cawdor Hotel. Leonard hugged and kissed us both, tears running down his and Beryl's cheeks, then climbed aboard and sat about half way back. He got off twice to hug us again before the conductor rang the bell and the bus trundled off,

Leonard waving and blowing kisses through the window. We waved until it turned the corner into Water Street and disappeared.

This visit is my entire recollection of Leonard. We never saw him again. And Beryl was pregnant for the second time.

Last Voyage

<u>Leonard to Beryl.</u>

Glasgow.
April 7 1944.

Cariad Annwyl,

Sorry there isn't time to write a proper letter now dear as we're sailing very shortly, but I hope to write a long letter before we finally leave this country.

The ship is a very good one, darling; far better than anything I have been on for many years, so that is some consolation. Also, she's not a V ship and is not engaged on any second front duties – another consolation. We expect to be away 3 or 4 months.

It was hopeless trying to fix up about the C&G exam. I saw the chief of W/T here and he'd written to them re sitting it in advance. They replied that they couldn't allow this procedure. The exam can only be sat on May 9 and they won't deviate from this rule whatever the circumstances. I have a letter of authority however, and if I'm in any place where the exam is being held on that date, I can sit.

Address letters to 1st RO, s/s Shahzada, c/o GPO, London (Air letters only).

Lots and lots of love to you both, and may God bless you and keep you very safe always,
Your very loving husband and Daddy,
Leonard. XXXX

After the rush to get him back to the *Shahzada*, it seems the sailing date was deferred. The National Archives Records show that she eventually sailed from Glasgow on the 13th, giving Leonard time to send one more letter:

<u>Leonard to Beryl.</u>   *Glasgow.*
                                            April 10 1944.

Cariad Annwyl,

I have been thinking of you during the holidays such a lot darling, (though I'm afraid that for both of us 'holidays' was quite the wrong word to use). How I wish I could have been home for those extra few days; you see, I know you were hoping as much as I was that it would have been possible for me to stay until the weekend.

Then too, beloved, I know the disappointing news about my exam will hurt, though I still have a chance in that direction. This uncertainty and the way it has dragged on now is very upsetting and you'll be as anxious I know for my sake as your own. After my outburst when I was home you'll probably be worrying about my feelings, darling, but fortunately getting it off my chest, and a world of good and substantial events have helped to make me feel lots better about it.

I mean, of course, my appointment to this ship. She's really a very good class ship with beautiful accommodation and attendance, and excellent food. I know I was appointed here as a result of the good work I did on my last ship and though I'm still rather disappointed at not being home over Easter, it has turned out far better than I expected.

As for the exam darling, well, if I can't sit this year, I can perhaps do the Intermediate and Final next year so that no time will be lost. I'd rather get one job over first of course, but by then perhaps things will be a lot better and maybe I can arrange leave off pay, or some such method to ensure that I'm ashore at the time, or I may even be able to arrange to get shore employment.

You really mustn't worry about my little bout of depression when I was home, cariad. That fortnight messing about and around the coast, probably the very large amount of work I did while the Captain was home, and of course dearest, the disappointment at not being able to see you, combined with the awful fact that I couldn't get all the leave that was due to me, got me down very badly and made me look at things at their very worst. They're not nearly as bad as that of course, and so long as I keep working hard for it I'm bound to land that shore job before very long.

And I will continue to work, sweetheart; you and little Clive mean so much to me that there's no obstacle going to prevent my coming home to you to share your lives and help and comfort you even as I want you to help and comfort me.

I arranged with the office to pay my salary through Head Office. The amount is £31-4-11 so you can expect a cheque any day now. If it doesn't come within a fortnight dear, you can write to Head Office about it, but the method is very reliable and I don't think it will be necessary.

I put £2-10-0 in the PO before leaving. I had to buy some things before joining as I can't live here as I did on the ships I've been used to lately. Here one wears uniform every day, shaves every day and uses a collar and tie. In fact you're always properly dressed. It will be a little more expensive I'm afraid, but my wages have been increased by £1-0-0 a month so I shan't lose out. I'll still have to buy some extra tropical kit, but I can get that abroad – it will be cheaper, and it won't require coupons.

Well, so much for business, darling. I can't tell you where we are going as this letter is almost certain to be censored; there's no harm though in saying that we're not engaged in any dangerous mission and we shan't be subjecting ourselves to any greater danger than was attached to all the other voyages I've made since the outbreak of war, and we definitely do not anticipate being away more than three or four months.

That, I know, sounds an awful long time and we're going to miss each other like anything. I shall write as often as I possibly can, dear, and the address for you to write to is:

> *s/s Shahzada,*
> *c/o GPO,*
> *London.*

Or   *s/s Shahzada,*
> *c/o Asiatic Steamship Co.,*
> *5-7 St Helen's Place,*
> *Bishopsgate, EC3.*

The latter is the Owner's address in case your letters are returned and you are asked to send them to the Owners. I think c/o GPO London is better because I got mail from them in every port on my last voyage.

I wish I were coming home and not going away now, dearest. I enjoyed my short leave such a lot that I wanted it to continue indefinitely. I haven't thanked you properly for making it such a happy time, but how can I do so now? There aren't any words to describe how much I enjoyed myself. Thank you very much, cariad fach, for making me feel so happy.

I'll try to make up for it all when we meet, darling. It will be mid summer then and we can have lots of nice times, you and I and Clive together. If I have a chance of inviting you aboard dear you must come because I know you'd have a nice time here with me; perhaps not quite up to the standard of the "Homeric" but very, very near it. I know that will mean leaving Clive, but it would do you a lot of good and I could come home and see him when we pay off. (I'm only assuming here that we'd call at another port in the UK before paying off, which isn't necessarily the case.)

Keep your little chin up while I'm away sweetheart. I love you from the bottom of my heart and am already looking forward to our next meeting. Give Clive a big hug from Daddy and tell him I'll be home soon again to play with him.

Lots and lots of love and kisses dear, and may God bless you both and keep you safe always.
Your very loving husband,
Leonard XXXX

Leonard to Beryl.

Aden.
May 12 1944.

Cariad Annwyl,
Thank you lots and lots for your two very nice letters dated April 10 and 18. They cheered me up immensely darling, though I was sorry to hear that you'd had German Measles.

No, dear, I didn't contract the complaint, and I'm feeling really fit and well again now. For the first time for many years I have been enjoying all my meals, feeling quite hungry at meal times and clearing my plate every time, instead of my usual drift, after ten days or so at sea, when I seem to lose my appetite completely and just nibble at my food.

It was hard lines, dearest, about my exam. As you can see, I just missed it by three days. I'll have to hope that third time will be lucky for the City and Guilds.

I think your idea of saving for holidays is a very good one, and your views re a second honeymoon are identical with mine. For over a year now I have been hoping that we could manage it sweetheart. You see, you deserve and need a complete change darling. That little holiday, such a happy one too, that we spent in Ardrossan, was a very long time ago, wasn't it, and since then you've been "keeping your nose steadily to the grindstone". You must have a change and I hope it will be when we next meet.

Then there's my love for you, dearest. I want to have you all to myself for a while to show you properly how much I love you. I do my best when I'm home but I never get the opportunity I really want. There's Clive, much as I love him, and the housework, my gardening and doing odd jobs, etc. It never gives us any time together. You know what I mean, cariad; no sooner do we get the day's work over than it's time to retire for the night. We're both generally too tired to enjoy properly the little that's left of the day. No sooner do we start settling down to an interesting companionship than it's time for supper, then washing up and so to bed.

That is what you feel too, isn't it darling? It doesn't make us unhappy because we're together and we're in love and just being near each other makes us happy. But the lack of change from constant routine makes us a bit stale, doesn't it? Makes us feel a lot older than our years, that feeling of tiredness and wanting to relax and rest just at the time when we are free and should be getting the most of the two or three hours of the day when there's just you and me together.

It affects you my dear, much more than it does me. At home I can be quite happy and I can honestly say I've enjoyed all my holidays with you. But then home is a complete change for me; for you it's no change at all except that loving me, making a fuss of me and having me with you makes you happy, darling.

Next time dearest we must try and get a few days together, then I'll try and show how very much I love you.

Lots and lots of love to both,
Your very loving husband and Daddy,
Leonard. XXXX

Leonard to Beryl.　　　　　　　　　　　*Bombay.*
May 24 1944.

Dearest,

It was nice to receive two lovely letters from you on our arrival here, cariad. The way you have expressed your love, and little Clive's love too, makes me feel very happy and very homesick, because there's so little I can do to repay you for your constant love and devotion.

The prospect of a little brother or sister for Clive has thrilled me very much darling. I wanted this to happen before Clive got very much older so that they'll be company for each other as they grow up. Gertie and I were always the best of friends and she's still my favourite sister. You see, there was too big an age difference between Maggie and myself. It will be good for Clive too, as he'll have a little responsibility and won't have all the attention. I'm afraid I spoil him when I'm home and make it difficult for you when I go away again.

I shall be thinking of you very much next month; longing that I could be home to spend the holiday with you. We haven't had summer days by the seaside together for ages, but I hope to manage it easily this year. More than ever now, dearest, I want to try and give you a thoroughly good holiday away from responsibility.

Look after yourself well now, and don't overdo things, and look forward to happy times when I return. Things are going all right out here at the moment and I should be away just about as long as I was last voyage. That's only a rough estimate of course, darling, and it may possibly be a little sooner.

I love you more than ever, sweetheart and words cannot describe how much I am missing you and thinking of you. I've only been able to post one letter to date but we only had the one opportunity. From now on though I can post fairly regularly, so you should find a big improvement in this respect.

I'm studying very hard these days so as to be quite ready for my exam when I get home. Every voyage I grow more discontented with having to leave you sweetheart, and I'll never be happy until I can get a shore job no matter how comfortable the ship I'm on.

I can never repay you properly for the happiness you've brought into my life, until I can be home always. You know that my heart is overflowing with love for you, cariad, but there's so few ways in which I can show it now. When this war's over there'll probably be more opportunity of arranging things to suit ourselves, then I shan't waste any time in trying to be with you always.

Meantime dearest, keep on loving me like you do now. God bless you both always.

Your very, very loving husband,
Leonard XXX

<u>Leonard to Beryl.</u>   *Karachi.*
                                                            May 27 1944.

Cariad Annwyl,

Just a few lines again, to let you know how much I am thinking of you and missing you sweetheart. Time seems to be passing very slowly these days and you are occupying my thoughts more and more every day.

As June approaches I keep longing that I could get home in time to spend the holidays with you, cariad. This month had such a lot to do with our good times in the past and I always feel very lonely if we can't be together then. I take comfort from it too because it always conveys to me the real turning point in my life. Our engagement did a lot of good all round if you remember, sweetheart. The best and sweetest little woman in the world promised to be mine, and it settled affairs at home in the only possible way that could be successful. I've always blessed that day, darling.

I have nothing new in the way of news for you. I still like the ship very much and feel in the best of health now. I'm feeding well, get plenty of rest and I think you'll notice a big improvement in my general condition when I come home.

I'm glad that Clive has cut those two back teeth and is helping you with the spring cleaning. He's a little dear, isn't he, with a lovely sweet nature even though he may be very naughty at times! How does he behave at meals now? Does he eat better since those teeth are through? I hope he does cariad, for your sake, as I know how very patient you are with him. Give him a nice big hug and kiss from me, darling.

Have a good time in Tresaith and try not to miss me too much. I shall be thinking of you dear and will be with you in spirit even if I'm not there myself. I love you more than I can express on paper darling, and when this war is over I hope to get a proper opportunity of showing it.

Meantime sweetheart, look forward to a nice time when I come home. I'm longing to give you a real holiday and am hoping to do it this time.

May God bless you and keep you always.
Lots and lots of love to you both,
Your very loving husband,
Leonard XXXX

Leonard to Beryl.   *Karachi.*
                                                        June 4 1944.

Sweetheart,
Many thanks for another nice letter received here. It cheered me up tremendously, cariad.

I was very glad to hear you are keeping fit and well, and that Clive is being a good boy. Glad too that you are missing me, dearest, though I don't want it to make you unhappy.

You see, darling, I'm missing you too, and I love you so

very much that I'm simply longing to be home again. The countryside will be looking its best now, with wild flowers and long grass everywhere, and it would be wonderful to be walking along the country lanes with you. It was just at this time of the year that we first started courting, when I kissed you for the very first time. It was the month when we became engaged, and the month when we spent that lovely holiday in Ardrossan. Can you wonder that I miss you so much sweetheart, when all these lovely memories haunt me every day?

When this war is over cariad, we'll visit these places again. For the present we must be patient and do all we can towards being ready for a shore job when the time comes.

Everything is going all right here so far and there's nothing new to add to what I've already written about prospects of my being home soon. I'm looking forward to seeing you again more than I've ever looked forward to it, dear. You see, this time I want it to be a holiday for you as well as for me.

I hope you'll have a nice time at Tresaith. I'll be thinking of you both all the time. Let's hope the weather is warm and sunny, and that you'll be able to spend most of the time out of doors. Clive will enjoy making sand castles on the beach, I know – I only wish I could be home to take him off your hands and let you rest and relax now, dear.

Look after yourself darling, and don't overdo things. Keep your little chin up because no matter where I am, I'm always thinking of you and loving you more and more every day. Time will pass quicker now that summer's here and very soon I hope we'll be together again.

Lots and lots of love to both, and may God bless you always.
Your loving husband,
Leonard XXXX

Leonard was far away when the D-Day operation of June 6, 1944 brought together the land, air and sea forces of the allied armies in what became known as the largest invasion force in human history. *Operation Overlord* delivered five naval assault divisions to the beaches of Normandy, France. The invasion force included 7,000 ships and landing craft manned by over 195,000 naval personnel from eight allied countries. Almost 133,000 troops from England, Canada and the United States landed on D-Day. Casualties from the three countries during the landing numbered 10,300. By June 30th, over 850,000 men, 148,000 vehicles, and 570,000 tons of supplies had landed on the Normandy shores. Fighting by the brave soldiers, sailors and airmen of the allied forces western front, and Russian forces on the eastern front, led to the eventual defeat of German Nazi forces.

<u>Leonard to Beryl.</u>   *Bombay.*
June 9 1944.

Beryl Darling,
It was so nice to receive another letter from you today. Up to date I've been doing very well and the postal service is so good these days that I'm almost tempted to write and thank the authorities for such an improvement!
Of course sweetheart, if you hadn't written so regularly, I shouldn't have been so well off, so thank you lots and lots for

keeping me well supplied with lovely letters. By now my letters should be arriving regularly, so I hope the service is just as good in your direction, and hope my letters are filling in the gap until I can be with you again.

I was very thrilled with news of Clive, that he was growing, was quieter and imaginative, and so on. Now that those teeth are through he'll probably improve a lot.

How I wish I could have accompanied you to Llan-grannog, darling. Yes, I know the road via Henllan well, as that was nearly always the route we used when I was a boy. The scenery around there is among the best in the country, especially at this time of the year and thinking of it, and of taking you there makes me feel quite young and romantic. It makes me feel very homesick too, cariad.

I always seem to long for you more at this time of the year than at any other, darling. We've spent some topping times together, haven't we? Cwm Valley must be marvellous now, and all the other places where we used to walk and gather flowers, where the smell of new-mown hay filled the air. Do you wonder that I miss you and long for you dreadfully?

Next year I hope we'll be able to spend some of these summer months together. It seems such a very long time since we last picked wild strawberries off the hedgerows, or sat down to a supper of nice fresh runner beans straight from the garden. It seems a very long time now, too, since I held you in my arms and told you I loved you. But I do love you dear, so much that it hurts.

Fancy Clive wanting a little brother! I suppose he feels then that there will always be someone around to play with. My hope is that it will be a little sister, too, but I won't hope

too much yet in case we're disappointed.
Loving you both lots and lots, and longing to be with you again. God bless you both always,
    Your very loving husband,
    Leonard XXXX

Tragedy

June 1944 brought the eagerly-awaited, restful holiday at the little seaside village of Tresaith that Beryl had been anticipating for so long. *The Hut* was a wooden building clad with pine weatherboard and creosoted black, with a tarred felt roof. It belonged to a Mrs Champion, and stood on a large grassy site which sloped towards the sea.

Tresaith. *The Hut* was the black building half way down on the right.

The big central living space was decorated with oars, fishing nets, cork and glass floats and other nautical items, and three bedrooms were divided off by partitions. Lighting was by candles or Tilley lamps, cooking was done on a temperamental Primus stove, water was drawn from a well and boiled, and there was an outdoor toilet a short distance away.

At the front a veranda faced due west with a panoramic view of the nearby beach and Cardigan Bay, where crabs, fish and sea anemones abounded in the rock pools, and the sea murmured a soothing lullaby at high tide. In the evenings the sun set over the sea, the rippling water reflecting the sky as it subtly changed through a palette of colours, from yellow to orange to a final dramatic deep red as the shadows lengthened and the sun slipped over the horizon. Beryl teased that if I listened carefully I'd hear it sizzling in the water as it set!

It was to have been the perfect place for adults and children to get away from the cares of the world. Beryl and I were first joined by her friend Rayda (who was also pregnant), her husband Jack, and daughter Pauline who was five months older than I, then various members of the family came and went during the course of the month.

Sadly, things began to go wrong almost immediately. Beryl miscarried.

<u>Beryl to Leonard.</u>

c/o The Hut,
Tresaith.
June 12 1944.

Cariad Annwyl,
It has been such a relief to get all your Air Letters and to hear you are safe and well and enjoying your food and new accommodation so much.
We do so wish you were here with us. It's a lovely airy hut,

with a very large lounge from which three bedrooms lead, and a very convenient scullery, and the hut contains everything under the sun, from soup dishes to walking sticks! I'm sure Gertie will love it here.

Well, sweetheart, I must come to the main point of this letter, and I hope you won't take it too much to heart. We lost our baby (the new one) last night. I had a miscarriage and am writing this in bed. I had carried it for nearly three months too, and am feeling very disappointed.

When I came over here I was feeling rather strained and ill, having rushed around to get everything washed and ironed and packed, and having developed swollen tonsils and a bit of a temperature, and then I noticed a slight discharge. Dr Budd told me to rest, and the discharge cleared up in about four days, and I felt a lot better. Four days later I went by bus to Cardigan, and when I arrived, there was a much heavier discharge starting, so I immediately went back to Newcastle-Emlyn and saw Dr Budd who told me to go to bed. Well, I had to walk here (Tresaith) from Aberporth, and Rayda and Jack were kindness itself, especially as Rayda shouldn't be on her feet too much just now.

I spent the whole day in bed, and just crossed the room in the evening to peep at Clive in bed. When I got back to bed I found myself losing lots of blood, just pouring out. Dr Budd brought Mother with him and the local Nurse came too, and they plugged me up with yards of lint. I lost a lot more blood last night, and the baby came away this morning.

I cried when I knew it was hopeless. Dr Budd says it is due to not relaxing enough, and that I take Clive too seriously. I'm in excellent physical health, but my nerves are very bad.

No pain.
 I love you dear, and am so very sorry.
  Your own
   Beryl XXXX

Beryl had developed German Measles - Rubella - early in her pregnancy. It is usually a mild illness but in a pregnant women the virus is likely to cause a miscarriage, or serious damage to the heart, brain, hearing and sight of the unborn child. Had she not miscarried, Beryl might have had a child seriously handicapped by congenital rubella syndrome. This is a recognised hazard nowadays, and prevented by immunisation, but Dr Budd apparently did not make the connection.

<u>Beryl to Leonard.</u>   *c/o The Hut,*
                                Tresaith.
                                June 16 1944.

Cariad,
 Just a note to let you know I'm getting on well, although I'm still in bed and feeling a bit weak from loss of blood. I will be getting up soon, I expect, but wish you were here as I'm a bit depressed over losing our little one. Dr Budd says I ought to have a good holiday away from Clive. The Nurse and Kitty think that dose of German Measles may have caused the miscarriage, as fevers often do. I had a high temperature at nights with it.
 The weather is still bitterly cold. Rayda and Mother are making me very comfortable and I ought not to be grumbling, dear, as I have all your love however far away you are. Kitty

offered to take Clive if I had to be nursed at Electra House but as it is, I'm staying quietly now. The change is doing Clive an enormous amount of good, and he eats a huge amount, but is rather fretful as he doesn't like me being in bed.

Dr Budd thought of sending me to hospital if things didn't go properly, but I think he is fairly satisfied that the whole of the placenta and embryo have come away.

The Newcastle-Emlyn Nurse, Kitty and Barbara came over on Tuesday. (We had to send for the Tanygroes Nurse on Sunday to save time and also I was in her district.) Everyone has been most kind, especially Rayda and Jack. Nurse says we will have to wait 6 months before I can think of having another baby, and I must build up my health properly beforehand.

I hear Gertie is having a lovely time at Harrogate and is staying another week.

Let's hope the war will be over soon and we'll be able to have a nice time together then. June is generally our lucky month, isn't it darling, although this time seems to have been an exception. But perhaps it was better to lose the baby now than to have miscarried later on. Shall be thinking of you all day on the 20th, beloved; as it is, you are constantly in my thoughts.

    Yn dy garu,
    Your own Beryl XXXX

Beryl to Leonard.
                                       c/o The Hut,
                                            Tresaith.
                                      June 18 1944.

Sweetheart Darling,

I've just been having a nice sleep and Nurse says I can get up for an hour tomorrow. Dr Budd has not been since Tuesday so you can see I am rapidly getting well. I can't help feeling miserable at times, wishing our little one had lived.

June is usually such a happy month for us both. I'm remembering the happy days we spent together in Ealing and wishing you were here now to comfort me a little. But I keep reading your letters and those are such a help, dear.

You know how I've been longing for a rest these many years; well, I've certainly had it, although not in the way I'd hoped. I feel perfectly relaxed now and am beginning to enjoy being here, although when I think of the baby my heart turns over. I'm longing to see you again, beloved.

Last night the sea looked so very beautiful – the sunset looked almost painted. I sat at the foot of the bed and wondered where you were, hoping you were well and safe. I hope conditions are still happy on the ship, dear, and that soon we shall be together for always.

Maggie Evans came here on Friday and is looking after Clive as well. Mother went back that night. Poor soul! I think she was tired out with the work and the excitement.

The holiday is doing Clive the world of good. He eats like a horse – I don't have to coax at all. He is such a happy little fellow these days and sends his Daddy love and kisses. You ought to see his lovely colour and flashing blue eyes! That's one worry off our minds anyway. He hasn't cut his last two teeth yet.

Now I must build up my health dearest, so that I can give you another healthy baby like Clive. You know how much I long for you and love you, beloved. Sometimes this intense yearning almost envelopes me. But one day I'm sure all the pain of partings will be over.

Do you remember the lovely Sunday we spent the year we were engaged, dear? It was a hot day and we had strawberries at Kew Gardens. Those days seem very far off, yet I am even happier now when you are home, sweetheart. I miss you so much when you are away because you are such a dear, kind husband.

God bless you, cariad. Praying for your swift return and loving you always,
    Your own
    Beryl XXXX

<u>Leonard to Beryl.</u>

Mormugao, Goa.
June 20 1944.

My Own Darling,

I have been thinking of you all day, dearest, firstly because it was on this date that you promised to be my dear wife. It was a time of great happiness for both of us, and I shall always bless the way things turned out for us then.

Secondly, darling, I'm afraid my news today is not very good. Our original plans have been changed and at the moment it looks very much as though I won't be home as soon as I'd expected to be. It's all very indefinite - all I can say at present is that I'll let you know later when to expect me home. There's nothing to worry about, darling, but it's an awful nuisance and very disappointing.

I got two lovely letters from you yesterday darling – thanks lots and lots for all the nice things you say about me. It was interesting to read about little Clive's progress. I'm glad that his teeth are through and that he's so much more comforting to you now, dear.

By the way darling I was told out here that Clive is going to have a little brother. The Chief Engineer does a little palm reading and is convinced our little family will be two boys. I don't believe him of course, and still hope it's going to be one of each.

You made my mouth water writing of tomatoes, etc. We're not badly off for food on this ship but I'd give a lot now for a big plate loaded with fried tomatoes or French beans fresh from the garden. I've been longing for the latter nearly as much as I long for you dearest, and believe me that's an awful lot!

I've been missing you really badly lately. Your lovely letters and a longing to be with you amidst all the beauty of the countryside makes me feel thoroughly homesick. Now today's news has made things worse and there's no describing my disappointment.

However, darling, I suppose we mustn't grumble. I've met lots of men out here who haven't seen their wives for five years. Colleagues stationed on the coast here are nearly as badly off and I'm very fortunate that I haven't been transferred. Things could be a lot worse than they are. At any rate darling, I'm looking forward to the delay being no more than a month or two.

I love you lots and lots cariad and will try to make up for it when we come home. Are you receiving my mail regularly now? I've written at least once a week and sometimes oftener, though we're rationed here to one Airmail letter card per week.

Give Clive a big kiss for me and tell him I'm very proud that he's being such a good boy. For you dearest, there's a great wealth of love in my heart though perhaps I can't express it on paper.

Lots of love, cariad,
Your very loving
Leonard XXXX

This was the last letter Beryl received from Leonard.

Beryl to Leonard.

The Hut,
Tresaith.
June 25 1944.

Sweetheart,

We are anxiously looking for letters from you but none have arrived for some time. Maybe you are on the way home, dear, and I would love that more than anything, as I need you more than ever now.

We have had glorious weather during the past week, but unfortunately it's raining again today. I'm feeling fairly well and am able to do my "whack" but I get bouts of weakness and depression thinking of what might have been if our little one had lived.

Dr Budd has given me a good iron tonic, and called to see me again yesterday. I have been up since Monday and am nearly back to normal once more. When I hear the weird and awful tales of other people's miscarriages, I realise how lucky I've been – apparently some poor women are ill for years whereas I am in good health already and in addition,

168

have had very little pain.

I'm afraid it will be an expensive month, dear. I've paid Nurse her fee of 15/- but still have Maggie Evans and the Dr to pay. Maggie is staying on a few days more and we are so glad to have her as she is excellent with the children and they love her company.

Poor old Dad Ball had another attack about a fortnight ago and mustn't do any gardening for a while. Also, Mr Swete fainted in church so poor Maggie has been worried to death and has lost 7 lbs in a very short while.

Gertie, Celia and Joanie are arriving on Saturday. I hope the weather will be fine for them.

Clive is very well but seems to have a bit of catarrh. I think those back teeth are almost through. He has awful obstinate moods. Mother and Dr Budd told me to give him a good smacking; I tried it the other day and really it didn't do an atom of good. It upset me thoroughly and poor old Clive howled terribly. I think his teeth worry him and then his nerves get upset and he doesn't quite know what to do with himself. Anyway, I don't intend smacking him again unless he does something really awful. He cried for you: "Daddy, I want my Daddy!"

He does love being here and flops in and out of the sea quite happily. He's got ever so sunburnt, too.

Dearest one, I hope you won't be terribly disappointed about the baby.

Do come home soon! I love you.

Your own

Beryl XXXX

The weather deteriorated. I remember torrential rain, with all of us cooped up in *The Hut* watching the downpour through the misted windows. Thunder crashed overhead and forked lightning stabbed through the clouds at the sea, reflected spectacularly in the steely-grey water. Totally oblivious to Beryl's concerns, my childish wish was to go and play on the beach, and I very much resented this imposition!

<u>Beryl to Leonard.</u>

The Hut,
Tresaith.
July 8 1944.

My dearest,

Just another line or two which I hope will help to shorten the distance between us. You have been so very much in my thoughts lately, dear, and I can't help wishing you were here at Tresaith, especially now that Gertie, Celia, Dad, Raymond and Joanie are here too. The weather is not at all good, but Dad and Raymond have managed to get hold of a fishing line and were down on the beach this morning setting it at 5 am. It's a good job Raymond was there too as Dad had come without his Identity Card, but fortunately Raymond had remembered his and produced it to the Coastguard.

I'm in very good health physically but have still a very low supply of nervous energy. I don't sleep very well; Clive snores like a piggery. He has a touch of catarrh. I didn't sleep in his room when Rayda was here but now I have to. I've tried blocking my ears with cotton wool but it's no use − the harsh sound penetrates everything! We have only a week again and were it not for the pleasant company and good sea air, I'd go home at once, but I feel the air is putting Clive right for the winter. Most people get a bout of insomnia here, as I believe the air is too bracing.

Gertie and I share the work – she makes the dinner one day, and I do it the next. Also I have my rations sent over and of course, there are enormous supplies from Llandysul!

Gertie sends her love (she is still as sweet as ever). Also Raymond, Dad and Joanie – the latter wants to know if you have managed to get her a doll!

Cariad, I am longing to be with you again and hope I'll be able to come up to you in Scotland. It would be nice to get completely away from Clive – darling though he is. Do you remember you remarked in one of your letters that I was too tired for anything after the day was done, and all we could do was sit by the fire – well, that's due to having a run-down nervous system, and I must try and repair that as quickly as possible.

I always love you, dearest, and long for you. Clive sends love and heaps of kisses.

> *Your own*
> *Beryl*
> *XXXX*

The *Shahzada* left Mormugao, Goa on July 6 1944 on her homeward run, heading west across the Arabian Sea bound for Aden. She was unescorted. On July 9, about 500 miles into the journey, Leonard was getting ready to end his watch at 10 pm. He would have been elated that they were on their way home at long last, thrilled at the thought of seeing his family again, and possibly looking forward to a hot cup of tea and a few chapters of a book before bedtime.

At 9.45 pm there was a big explosion forward. The ship shuddered and began to take on water and sink as she was holed by a torpedo from the German submarine *U-196*. It was everyone's worst nightmare come true. There was a heavy swell, a moderate gale blowing, no moon, and it was raining.

Leonard remained at his post, frantically sending the SOS distress signal with their position over and over again, as the doomed ship listed and foundered. A survivor later recounted that the order to abandon ship had been passed by word of mouth and not signalled on the steam whistle. Confined in the radio cabin and intent on his task, Leonard may not have heard the order and probably left it too late to escape.

As a result of his gallant act of heroism, fifteen of the crew were rescued by the British *Changon* and landed at Bombay on July 17, and sixteen were rescued by the Swedish *Magna* and landed at Aden on July 21. A further 21 reached Goa in the lifeboats on July 18. In all, 52 crew survived but Leonard was lost, together with the Captain, the 2nd and 3rd Radio Officers, 33 other crew members, and nine gunners.

Thus all the yearnings, dreams, hopes, plans and expectations of a happy future by Leonard and Beryl were abruptly snuffed out and brought to nothing..

Leonard didn't receive the news about Beryl's miscarriage. His last agonised, drowning thoughts would have been about her and their children, born and unborn, and the terrible realisation that they would never see each other again.

Meanwhile Beryl, unaware of the disaster that had ended Leonard's life, continued writing letters that the man she had loved would never read. All the letters she wrote from Tresaith were eventually returned marked *Deceased* in red ink.

Beryl to Leonard.

c/o Electra House,
Newcastle-Emlyn.
July 19 1944.

Cariad,

From the address on the outside you will see I'm with Mother at Electra House, having returned from Tresaith on Saturday. Clive is behaving fairly well here but wants to go back to "his own house" which is at the moment occupied by my cousin Vera and family. I'm glad to be with Mother at the moment as I'm not feeling too strong, but Dr Budd is very pleased with my progress, so there's no need to worry, sweetheart.

I've just had a phone call saying Gertie had to take Celia home from the sea as it hadn't been suiting her. She's had a high temperature and a rash. Clive hasn't been too good lately, so I hope he's not developing the same thing.

The weather has turned out very hot dear, but not really fine – it's too sultry.

Clive is eating cornflakes very tidily as I write, but has an awful snuffle. The last two back teeth are not through yet. He got his hand caught between the chain and the cog of Dad's bicycle this morning. Dad had to take the chain right off before we could release his little hand. Fortunately he wasn't hurt at all, only frightened.

Raymond came over to Tresaith for the second week of our stay, and Maggie sent some wonderful food over – raspberries and peas – you should have seen Clive tucking in! If you had been there, everything would have been perfect, sweetheart.

Your further letter came yesterday, cariad, for which many thanks. What a pity you are delayed again! Just as I was beginning to prepare to see you soon, this very disappointing news comes through, but no doubt it's much worse for you than for me, as you are anxious about me if you have had my June letters.

Oh cariad! Why are we kept apart so long, so often? I'm longing to see you so very much and I know you are yearning for us all and your home, dearest.

Clive keeps asking for his Daddy and sends heaps of love. These are Clive's kisses – I'm guiding his little hand   XXXX

With all my love,
Your own
Beryl XXXX

Beryl to Leonard.   *c/o Electra House,*
                                          Newcastle-Emlyn.
                                          July 23 1944.

Cariad,

Just another line to say how much I'm missing you and thinking of you. I've read your last letter over and over again and am sorry you are going to be delayed. I feel I want to comfort you and to be comforted over the loss of our baby, and hope you won't be unduly upset when you get the news of my miscarriage. I feel you are putting your mind a lot on the coming of our second little one and that the disappointment will be all the more.

I am feeling a bit weak lately but everyone thinks I look well, so I am really improving although it takes time.

Clive is very trying lately and I don't get as much sleep as I ought to. It is so difficult being in Electra House, although it is a great relief having Mother and Dad to take Clive off my hands occasionally.

He has taken to waking in the nights and is generally disobedient, just when I want him to be good. I believe he is cutting the last two molars, and I do hope his behaviour will improve once they come through.

I would give anything to have a month or two away from him if I knew he would be well cared for and happy. However, I expect he'll improve once he finishes teething. Gertie has offered to take Clive up there when I want to visit you, dear, so I'm hoping this will be possible.

We are looking everywhere for a furnished house for my cousin Vera and her three children. At the moment they are at 4 Castle Street but are paying me 30/- a week. The arrangement is only temporary and I have explained you like to come home to your own home, so they will have gone by the time you are next here, sweetheart. The arrangement suits me at the moment as I would get very depressed if just living with Clive over there.

The weather is lovely and fine this evening. I've been picking peas in the garden here, and somehow this took me back to our courting days when you used to visit me at Electra House.

I am just turning in to dream of you, beloved, and with the hope that the days and hours which separate us will fly, and that you'll come soon.

> *All my love,*
> > *God bless you dearest,*
> > *Your own*
> > > *Beryl XXXX*

Finally, the devastating news that Leonard was missing reached Beryl. A friend of hers told me some years ago that she had met Beryl coming out of the Newcastle-Emlyn post office sobbing uncontrollably. She believed she'd received a telegram with the tragic information and had just phoned for clarification. The Admiralty had also sent her a letter.

From the Asiatic Steam Navigation Company Ltd.

5&7 St Helen's Place,
Bishopsgate,
London EC3.

Mrs Beryl Ball
4 Castle Street
Newcastle-Emlyn   *August 3 1944.*

Dear Madam,
We acknowledge receipt of your letter of 1st instant re Radio Officer LF Ball. The only information we can give you in addition to that which you have already received from Admiralty, is that the survivors, representing about half the crew, have been landed in India and unfortunately none of the Radio Officers has reported so far.
You will, of course, be advised by Admiralty immediately any further information comes to hand, and in the meantime we desire to express our sincere sympathy with you in your anxiety.
Yours faithfully,
pp Asiatic Steam Navigation Co. Ltd.
WD Howes,
Director.

<u>A final, heart-rending letter from Beryl to Leonard.</u>

c/o Electra House,
Newcastle-Emlyn.
August 6 1944.

My own dear, dear husband,

It is so peaceful, sitting here in the sunshine, that I cannot believe the dreadful news that your ship has been sunk, and you haven't yet been reported among the survivors.

How I pray for your safety, beloved, and that good news won't be long in coming. Clive has begged me to write you this morning and to send love and kisses to dear Daddy.

Oh cariad, if only I knew you were safe! You know, I never minded the loneliness, and anxiety, and waiting, and the lack of news, so long as I knew you were safe. But I feel we are all in God's hands, beloved, every moment we breathe, and that wherever you are, you are in His keeping. We trust in Him whatever happens. Oh my dear, dear one, how I wish you were here now! What wouldn't I give for a glimpse of your dear, kind face?

When you come back dearest, there's going to be no more partings if I can help it. You are going to stay with us always and earn those well-deserved happy hours at home. Cariad, even if I have to work harder than I've ever worked, I'll help you with a little business if necessary. I cannot believe you are not safe and well – your dear presence is always beside me, beloved one, and wherever you are, I know you are in God's keeping. I will be very patient until I hear good news which must come, dear heart.

May God in His infinite mercy and love protect you

wherever you are.
Writing soon again,
Your very own
Beryl XXXX

<u>Eye-witness account to Captain Hamilton's wife from a survivor.</u>

14 Meadowcroft Crescent,
Edinburgh 8.
October 10 1944.

Dear Mrs Hamilton,

In answer to your letter which I received today, please accept my sympathy in what must be for you a very anxious time.

I will try now, Mrs Hamilton, to fill in some of the details for you regarding the sinking.

We left Mormugao on July 6 and were torpedoed on the 9th at about 9.45 pm, our position being at that time approximately Lat 15°30'N, Long 66°E. There was a moderate gale blowing from the south west and the night was dark, with no moon.

When the ship was struck the other apprentice and I went up to the bridge where Captain Hamilton, accompanied by the 1st, 2nd and 3rd Officers were. After being there for about eight minutes, Captain Hamilton instructed us to go to our boat stations and stand by. About 10 minutes after, the 2nd Officer acting on the Captain's instructions also came on to the boat deck, and I assume the 1st and 3rd Officers stayed on the bridge with Captain Hamilton, as I saw no sign of them on the boat deck.

Approximately 10 minutes later the abandon ship order came, which was passed by word of mouth and not signalled on the steam whistle. At this time the ship had a list of about 30° to port and was still under way.

When I eventually got into a lifeboat along with the 2nd Officer, the other apprentice, a gunner and two Indian seamen, the ship was still above water but some way off, and there were three other lifeboats in sight. In my opinion the ship took 15 to 20 minutes after the "abandon ship" to sink therefore giving ample time for everybody to at least get into the water and get clear of the ship before she finally sank.

Captain Hamilton's boat was not on the boat deck but was on the deck beside his cabin, which was one deck below the bridge, so I had no other opportunity of seeing him after I left the bridge.

As far as I know, no one was injured by the explosion which occurred well forward.

Other people I remember seeing before the "abandon ship" was given were the Chief, 2nd, 3rd and 5th Engineers, the 2nd and 3rd Radio Officers, and some gunners. These people were all on the boat deck, and all were wearing life jackets.

The 4th Engineer, Mr Russell, was on watch in the engine room at this time, but was apparently unhurt as I spoke to him through the voice pipe on the bridge. He said he needed some help down below as most of the engine room staff had gone up on deck.

The 1st Radio Officer, Mr Ball, was in the Wireless Cabin sending out distress signals when I left the bridge.

When we were picked up we compared our position at the

time the ship was sunk, with the position where we were rescued, and we found that we had drifted in a southerly direction towards the Laccadive Islands some 60 miles after being adrift two days. These islands were about 500 miles distant.

I hope, Mrs Hamilton, that this letter will bring you a little satisfaction. If at any future date I get to know anything more definite, I will be only too pleased to let you know at once.

Please don't hesitate to write if I can be of any further assistance to you.

Yours very sincerely,

Hugh Watson (Apprentice on s/s Shahzada.)

From the Asiatic Steam Navigation Company Ltd.

5&7 St Helen's Place,
Bishopsgate,
London EC3.

Mrs Beryl Ball
4 Castle Street,
Newcastle-Emlyn.   *October 31 1944.*

Dear Madam,

s/s Shahzada.

A report on the loss of the above steamer has now been received from the Managing Agents in India, Messrs Turner, Morrison and Co Ltd.

The steamer sailed from Mormugao for Aden on July 6, and on July 9 at about 9.45 pm, when approximately 500 miles west of Mormugao, was torpedoed. There was a rough sea with heavy swell and rain squalls at the time. The ship was hit on the port side, between No 1 and No 2 holds, and after remaining on a level keel for about ten minutes, proceeded to settle down by the head.

After SOS messages had been sent out, an order to abandon ship was given, and six life boats were launched, of which Nos 2 and 4 subsequently landed in India and the occupants of Nos 5 and 6 were rescued at sea. These four boats remained anchored in the vicinity overnight, but next morning there was no sign of the steamer. It seems that of the other two, the motor boat (No 3) broke adrift after being launched with nobody in it, whilst No 1 boat was last seen hanging on end from one davit.

Apart from the four life boats accounted for, the only news has been of one raft identified by the registration number, washed up on the Goa coast, with two unidentified bodies in it, one European and one Indian, which were immediately interred.

The survivors reported safe are eight Europeans and forty-four Indians, and included in the missing forty-four members of the crew are the Master (Captain AS Hamilton), four Engineers, three Radio Officers and nine Gunners. After a lapse of more than three months, it appears that hope of there being any other survivors must be abandoned.

Our Managing Agents in India join with us in expressing sincere sympathy to all relatives of missing officers and seamen.

Yours faithfully,
pp Asiatic Steam Navigation Co Ltd,
WD Howes
Director.

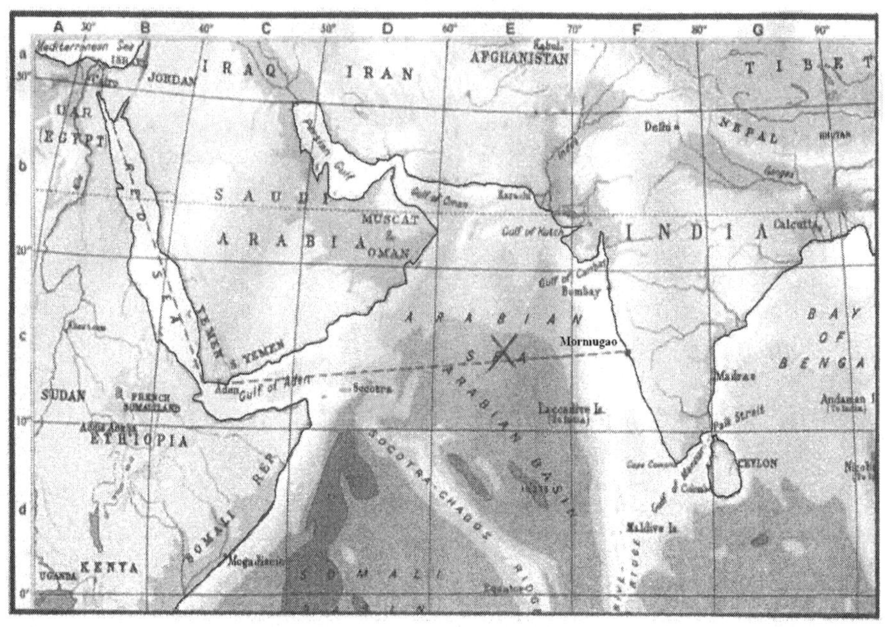

Map showing where the *Shahzada* was torpedoed and sunk.

<u>From The Marconi International Marine Communication Co. Ltd.</u>

Marconi House,
Chelmsford.

Mrs B Ball,
4 Castle Street,
Newcastle-Emlyn.   *November 2 1944.*

Dear Madam,
    We deeply deplore the necessity of referring to previous correspondence in connection with the loss of the vessel upon

which your husband, Mr LF Ball, was serving, and it is with profound regret we have to inform you that a communication has now been received from the owners in which they advise us that, in view of the length of time which has elapsed since the vessel was lost, they can hold out no further hope of there being any more survivors from the ill-fated vessel.

It is our painful duty, therefore, to inform you that your husband is considered to have lost his life with the vessel on July 9 1944.

In passing this sad news to us, the owners state that the vessel sailed from Mormugao for Aden on July 6, and at about 9.45pm on July 9, when about 500 miles west of Mormugao, she was torpedoed. At the time there was a rough sea with a heavy swell and rain squalls.

Distress signals were sent out, and an order to abandon ship given. Four of the ship's lifeboats, containing 52 survivors, eventually made landfall, but since the time of the incident, no news has been received of the missing members of the crew.

The Chief Officer reports that your husband was on watch in the Wireless Room sending the distress signals, and the Chief Officer was under the impression that your husband left the ill-fated boat with the Captain who, we regret to say, has also been reported as having lost his life.

The lifeboats from the vessel remained anchored in the vicinity overnight, but the next morning there was no sign of the steamer or of any member of the crew, other than those who were safe in the boats.

Our Chairman desires us to convey to you his deepest sympathy in the great loss you have been called upon to bear, and we trust it will afford you some measure of comfort in your great sorrow to know that during the time your husband was employed by us he carried out his duties to our entire satisfaction, and his conduct was all that could be desired.

We feel sure also that you will like to know that your husband is numbered amongst the heroes who have so nobly upheld the traditions which have existed in the British Mercantile Marine for so many generations.

The owners and Managing Agents of the vessel in India desire us to express to you their deepest sympathy in your great bereavement.
Yours faithfully,
H. Alan de Velde,
Deputy to the Managing Director.

The Aftermath

Normally, when a person dies, the deceased is visited, mourned and laid to rest with the appropriate rituals and commemoration. This helps the grieving process, and comforts and enables their loved ones to achieve "closure". In Beryl's case this never happened. The "not knowing" considerably prolonged the agony of losing Leonard.

Firstly, his body was not recovered and so the possibility that he had survived lingered on for a long time. There had been instances of shipwrecked mariners reappearing long after all hope had been lost, and Beryl with total faith in her God, flatly refused to believe that Leonard would not come home, and that their hopes and plans for the future would not be realised. For my third birthday on Nov 3 1944, Maggie made a beautiful iced fruit cake – goodness knows where she got the ingredients – and I remember Beryl putting a huge piece of it in a cake tin "for Daddy, when he comes home". It stayed in the pantry until it grew mouldy.

Secondly, the report in the letter from the Asiatic Steam Navigation Co Ltd, that a raft from the ship, with the bodies of a European and an Indian on it, had been washed up on the Goa coast, preyed on Beryl's mind. She wanted the bodies exhumed, as she felt Leonard could easily be identified because one of his top front teeth had been chipped by a cricket ball. Dr Budd advised her to "let it go" but that was easier said than done.

Thirdly, Jack, though a very competent engineer, was enthralled by the quackery of dowsing (also called water divining). He had found supplies of water for grateful people in unlikely places around Newcastle-Emlyn, and Beryl had great faith in his abilities. However, Tom told me that his credulity had been severely strained when he saw Jack dangling a pendulum over a map of the Indian Ocean, which evidently led to the following correspondence:

<u>Jack to Beryl.</u>

Electra House,
Newcastle-Emlyn.
November 9 1944.

My Dear Beryl,

Don't let the letter you had from the Chief Officer (Mother has told me of it) get you down. Many an event has happened after slender chances.

I have reason to believe that Leonard is alive, but marooned and at present away from communications.

I am cautious about raising your hopes unduly, as he may not yet be out of danger, but when the full story becomes known I think it will be found that he is alive at the present date.

So keep your chin up, kid – my margin is within the next eight months before I shall begin to lose hope.

With fondest love and a hug for the boy,
    Yours always,
      Dad XX

Jack's advice was obviously given with the best of intentions, but totally misguided.

From the British Red Cross Society; Wounded, Missing and Relatives Department.

7 Belgrave Square,
London SW1.

Mrs B Ball,
4 Castle Street,
Newcastle-Emlyn.   *December 8 1944.*

Dear Mrs Ball

We have received your letter of December 5 regarding your husband, 1st Radio Officer Leonard Frederick Ball. It would be of assistance to us in our enquiries regarding him if you would kindly send us the latest official notification you have received about him, or an exact copy of it.

In regard to the questions you have asked in your letter, we are glad to give you such information as we have. We have not received names of prisoners of war who may recently have been captured by the Japanese. During the past year a postcard from the prisoner of war to his next of kin has been the most usual first notification of his capture.

The Service by which the Japanese Government promised to allow each prisoner of war in their hands to send a cable to his next of kin is nominally now in operation, but up to the present, no cables have been received. Had your husband succeeded in reaching the shores of Arabia or the East coast of South Africa, he would have been in British territory, and free to make himself known, and to make use of any means available for communication with this country.

We are sorry we cannot send you any more definite news concerning your husband, but would assure you again that

should any reach us from any source, we would let you know immediately.
With our renewed sympathy,
Yours sincerely
Margaret Ampthill (Chairman.)

From the Ministry of War Transport.

Berkeley Square House,
London W1.

Mrs Beryl Ball,
4 Castle Street,
Newcastle-Emlyn.   *January 22 1945.*

Dear Madam,
   I am writing in reply to your letter of January 11 enquiring about your husband Mr Leonard Frederick Ball, 1st Radio Officer s/s "Shahzada".
   The "Shahzada" was torpedoed and sunk on July 9 1944. It has been reported that only four boats got away from the ship and all those with their occupants have been accounted for. Another boat was lowered but up-ended, fell into the water and, the painter having been carried away, the boat drifted away empty.
   The members of the crew were interviewed at the Admiralty and from their reports it appears unlikely that another boat could have got away from the vessel. The Admiralty state further that after this lapse of time, it is thought that had any survivors arrived in the Laccadive Islands they would by now have been found.

I am most sorry that it is not possible to give you better news and I have been asked by the Minister of War Transport to convey to you an expression of his deep sympathy.
Yours faithfully,
MP Hubbard.

<u>NEWCASTLE-EMLYN RADIO OFFICER'S SAD FATE.</u> In the latest list of war casualties published by the Ministry of War Transport appears the name of First Radio Officer Leonard Frederick Ball, 4 Castle Street, Newcastle-Emlyn. The ship on which he was serving was sunk on July 9 last, and four of the five boats have been accounted for, having travelled 500 miles. Mr Ball, who had been at sea for 15 years, was last seen at his post sending out distress calls – a fact of which his wife, Mrs Beryl Ball, who refuses to give up hope, is justifiably proud. Lieutenant Ball was the eldest son of Mr FH Ball and the late Mrs Ball, Rock House, Llandysul where he was educated at the National and County Schools. (*Cardigan and Tivy-Side Advertiser*, March 2 1945.)

In the kindly manner of small communities, relatives, neighbours and friends rallied round to cheer Beryl and heal her sorrow; understandably it took time for this to happen. At night she would spend long periods on her knees, praying earnestly at her bedside before sleep; other times she would weep uncontrollably and hug me silently. I shared her sadness but was too young to understand its full implications.

Beryl eventually came to accept that Leonard would not be coming home, yet for years afterwards occasionally gave the impression that she expected him sometime, probably as a result of being used to his long absences and the lack of closure I mentioned earlier. She never associated with another man – Leonard had been all-in-all to her and no-one else could ever compare.

Annie and Jack lived quite near us and I spent a lot of time with them when Beryl needed a bit of peace or some child minding. I started school in May 1945, just before VE Day when the War ended in Europe, and often went to *Electra House* for tea after school. Annie was kind and motherly; Jack became my father figure. He was always doing things which interested me and I learned a lot of electrical and mechanical principles from him over the years, even though he was a gruff old Victorian who believed that children should be seen and not heard!

Beryl was a good and loving mother, and supported and encouraged all my interests. We enjoyed a close relationship, and of course I thought she was the best Mum in the world. In 1946 she returned to work, as a secretary/bookkeeper at the Cawdor Hotel in Newcastle-Emlyn. Throwing herself into an active social life, she involved herself with a local drama group, the Attic Players; the Mothers' Union; the Women's Institute and the Chamber of Trade.

War memorials bearing Leonard's name were unveiled at Newcastle-Emlyn, Llandysul Church and Llandysul County School. Every July, Beryl arranged the altar flowers in Holy Trinity Church on the Sundays before and after the 9th in remembrance of him. A small parcel arrived one morning in 1951 and Beryl opened it, becoming tearful when she found it contained Leonard's war medals and ribbons.

In 1955 we travelled to London to be present at the opening of the 1939-45 extension to the Merchant Navy War Memorial on Tower Hill on November 5. Leonard's name appears on panel 95 together with those of the other British crew of the *Shahzada* who were lost. The ceremony was performed by our new Queen who had been reigning for less than four years. I remember being very thrilled to see her.

The Merchant Navy Memorial Panel on Tower Hill, London.

Also in 1955, Beryl changed her job and became a medical secretary at the West Wales General Hospital in Carmarthen. She remained there until 1963, when she moved to Hertford where I was living, and worked as personal secretary to several surgeons at hospitals in the area until 1971.

Jack died in 1965; Annie sold *Electra House* and moved to 4 Castle Street as had been her original intention. She divided her time between her home, Hertford, and Tom and Kitty's home in Stourport-on-Severn. I left to travel to Australia the same year; Beryl continued working until 1971 when she turned 60, then returned to Newcastle-Emlyn to take care of Annie there. Annie died at the end of 1972.

In retirement, Beryl kept up her social activities, and we exchanged several visits between Newcastle-Emlyn and Australia over the years. In 1993 she suffered a dizzy spell when returning home from shopping, fell over in the street, and was taken into *Cartref Glyn Nest,* a local retirement home, to recover. She decided of her own accord to stay there, which was a great relief to me as she was developing dementia and I was living too far away to visit very often.

Beryl's letters to me ceased abruptly when she had a mini stroke; her condition gradually deteriorated further. She had difficulty remembering who I was when I visited, and confused me with her brother Tom.

In mid-1998 she was moved to a nursing home at Horeb. She died at the end of that year, and was buried in the grounds of Holy Trinity Church, Newcastle-Emlyn, where she had been christened, confirmed and married, where she had played the organ, and where she had worshipped her God unfalteringly. The gravestone commemorates Leonard too, and for their epitaph I chose the first line of a well-known Welsh hymn, *Dyma gariad fel y moroedd* - Here is a love (as vast) as the oceans.

It seems fitting.

In Memoriam - Merchant Navy 1939-1945.

No cross marks the place where now we lie;
What happened is known but to us.
You asked, and we gave our lives to protect
Our land from the enemy curse.
No Flanders Field where poppies blow;
No Gleaming Crosses, row on row;
No Unnamed Tomb for all to see
And pause - and wonder who we might be.
The Sailors' Valhalla is where we lie
On the ocean bed, watching ships pass by;
Sailing in safety now through the waves,
Often right over our sea-locked graves.
We ask you just to remember us.   *P. Andrews.*

Appendix

The *Shahzada* was a steam merchant vessel of 5,454 tons owned by the Asiatic Steam Navigation Company, London. She was built by Lithgows in Glasgow, and completed and launched in June 1942.

Her first voyage in October 1942 took her to New York, Cuba, Trinidad, Durban, Colombo then back to London via Durban and Freetown by July 1943, carrying general cargo.

http://www.clydesite.co.uk/clydebuilt/viewship.asp?id=18338

The *Shahzada* in her wartime grey camouflage.

The second trip commencing in August 1943 was via Gibraltar, Port Said, Suez, Aden, Karachi, Bombay, Colombo, Trincomalee and Madras to Calcutta, then home via Madras and Colombo, again carrying general cargo. On the way to Aden she rescued the entire crew (49) of the Liberty ship *Samouri,* which had been sunk by *U-188* on January 26 1944 near Socotra Island in the Gulf of Aden, and landed them at Aden before continuing to Britain via Suez and the Mediterranean.

Captain Allan Scott Hamilton

Leonard joined the *Shahzada* in April 1944 for her third and last journey, via the Mediterranean and Port Said, Suez, Aden, Karachi, Bombay to Mormugao. She tarried in Karachi for ten days, Bombay for three weeks and Mormugao for two weeks, loading and unloading cargoes at those ports. On her last voyage home she was carrying a cargo of 5,000 tons of groundnuts and 98 crew.

The Master (who also lost his life with the ship) was Allan Scott Hamilton, aged 39.

***U-196*, the German submarine** which sank the *Shahzada*, was launched at Bremen on April 24 1942. Leaving Kiel on March 13 1943 under the command of *Kapitänleutnant* Eitel-Friedrich Kentrat, she completed the longest patrol made by a submarine during World War 2, spending 225 days at sea.

Photo: uboat.net

Kapitänleutnant Eitel-Friedrich Kentrat

During that time she sailed all the way around the coast of South Africa and sank two British Merchant ships, the *Nailsea Meadow* and the *City of Oran*, in the Indian Ocean before returning to Bordeaux.

It was on her second patrol, leaving Bordeaux on March 16 1944 bound for the Far East, that she sank the *Shahzada* in the Arabian Sea. When she arrived in Penang on August 10 that year, Kentrat was replaced.

Kentrat served in Japan to the end of the war, and returned to Germany in October 1947 after over two years in captivity. He died in 1974 aged 67.

On November 30 1944, *U-196* left Java with *Oberleutnant zur See* Werner Striegler in command. She was assigned to refuel a sister U-boat in the Indian Ocean but disappeared without trace and was listed as missing in the Sunda Straits south of Java about December 12 1944. Her wreck has never been found, or the cause of her disappearance determined. She carried 65 crew.

Because *U-196* suffered an unknown fate, several conspiracy myths about her disappearance have been spawned and can be found on the Internet. One claims that her wreck has been found near the New Zealand coast, and that she was used to transport fleeing Nazis and a hoard of gold (payment for uranium) from Japan to New Zealand, then scuttled. Another claims that she was used to convey escaping Nazis to Chile in South America.

My personal opinion is that these are just myths. The most likely explanation is that she hit some unexpected large underwater obstacle near Java and was fatally damaged.

German Intelligence from Goa. Until 1961, Goa was a Portuguese state on the Indian sub-continent, and took a neutral position during the War. The Germans had a secret transmitter on the *Ehrenfels*, one of their ships interned in Mormugao harbour, whose purpose was to guide the U-boats to strike Allied shipping in the Indian Ocean.

The transmitter had to be silenced, and the job was done by an unlikely group of retired civilian bankers, merchants and solicitors from 1,400 miles away in Calcutta, the remains of an old territorial unit called *The Calcutta Light Horse.* The tiny force attacked and sank the *Ehrenfels* at anchor on the night of May 9, 1943. This enterprise, known as *Operation Creek*, was a secret for more than twenty-five years.

Their remarkable achievement is related in *The Boarding Party* by James Leasor, which was later filmed as *The Sea Wolves.* The destruction of the transmitter removed its threat to the Allied shipping for a while. Was it replaced by the time the *Shahzada* was torpedoed? *U-196* was ostensibly on her way to the Far East, which should have taken her much farther south than where she encountered the *Shahzada*, unless she had received instructions to divert her course, from a shore-based informant.

Alan Smith, Radio Officer. Whilst searching the Internet for further details of the *Shahzada*, I found a reference to Alan Smith, who had also been a Radio Officer on the ship, and was able to contact him by email. Alan, fresh out of the Colwyn Bay Wireless College, was given his first appointment as 3rd Radio Officer on the *Shahzada* on her second voyage in August 1943. He sailed with her as far as Calcutta before being transferred to another ship.

Now in his late 80s at the time of writing and living near Lima, Peru, Alan and I still correspond. It seems extraordinary to be in touch with someone who sailed with Captain Hamilton, and operated the same Morse key that Leonard used to send the SOS, all those 70 years ago.

Glossary of Welsh terms.

Annwyl. — Dear.

Bach, fach. — Little.

Byddaf i'n meddwl amdanat ti yr oll amser, ac yn edrych ymlaen am y tro nesa'. — I'll be thinking of you all the time, and looking forward to the next time.

Cariad, gariad. — Darling, love.

Cariad fach, rwy'n meddwl cymaint amdanat ti y dyddiau 'ma! — Little darling, I'm thinking so much about you these days!

Cariad fach, rwy'n hiraethu ar dy ôl yn ofnadwy. — Little darling, I'm longing for you terribly.

Cofion gorau. — Best remembrances.

Diolch yn fawr iawn am yr amser rhagorol ces i gyda ti, cariad. — Thank you very much indeed for the excellent time I had with you, darling.

Hen Wlad fy Nhadau. — Land of my Fathers (Welsh National Anthem.)

Rwy'n dy garu yn fwy nag erioed. — I love you more than ever.

Tyrd adre'n gloi. — Come home quickly.

Yn dy garu. — Loving you.

Ysgol ar y Bryn. — School on the Hill.